illustrations in children's books

literature for children

Pose Lamb
Consulting Editor
Purdue University

Storytelling and Creative Drama—*Dewey W. Chambers, University of the Pacific, Stockton, California*

Illustrations in Children's Books—*Patricia Cianciolo, Michigan State University*

Enrichment Ideas—*Ruth Kearney Carlson, California State College at Hayward*

History and Trends—*Margaret C. Gillespie, Marquette University*

Poetry in the Elementary School—*Virginia Witucke, Purdue University*

Its Discipline and Content—*Bernice Cullinan, New York University*

Children's Literature in the Curriculum—*Mary Montebello, State University of New York at Buffalo*

illustrations in children's books

PATRICIA CIANCIOLO
Michigan State University

Pose Lamb
Consulting Editor
Purdue University

WM. C. BROWN COMPANY PUBLISHERS
Dubuque, Iowa

Printed in the United States of America

contents

foreword

This series of books came to be because of the editor's conviction that most textbooks about literature for children had not been written for elementary teachers, regardless of the anticipated audience suggested by the titles. The words, *Literature for Children*, preceding each individual title indicate not only the respect for the field held by the authors and the editor but our evaluation of the importance of this type of literature, worthy of consideration along with other categories or classifications of English literature. However, it is *what happens* through books, and the *uses* of literature which are of concern to the authors of this series, as well as the provision of an historical perspective and some knowledge of the writer's and the illustrator's crafts. Our work, then, is directed primarily to the elementary classroom teacher who wants to design and implement an effective program of literature for children.

Because entire books have been devoted to specific topics, for example, the history of literature for children, it is hoped that such topics are covered in greater depth than usual. They are not merely books *about* children's literature; the focus in this series is on helping teachers see what literature for children has been, the direction or directions pointed by scholars in the field, and some ways in which a teacher can share with children the excitement and joy of reading. The authors have tried to share with teachers and prospective teachers their enthusiasm for children's literature, today's and yesterday's; for an unenthusiastic teacher, though well-informed, will not communicate enthusiasm to his pupils.

The author of each book was selected, first because he has demonstrated this enthusiasm in his teaching and writing, and secondly because of his competence in the field of children's literature in general. It is hoped that the thoroughness and depth with which each topic has been explored and the expertise which each author has brought to a topic in which he has a particular interest will serve as sufficient justifications for such a venture.

Children's literature courses are among the most popular courses in the professional sequence at many colleges and universities. It is rewarding and exciting to re-enter the world of literature for children, to experience again the joy of encountering a new author or of renewing acquaintance with a favorite author or a character created by an author.

The editor and the authors of this series have tried to capture the magic that is literature for children and to provide some help for teachers who want to share that *magic with children.*

Art and design, as they are reflected in books for children and adolescents, are fascinating fields of study. Illustrators do not agree as to the best answers to these questions, and the readers of this book probably won't agree either!

> Should the art in children books be representational or abstract? How does one decide what techniques, what media are most appropriate for conveying the artist's and writer's messages?

> Are illustrations in childrens books primarily adornments, an attractive and enticing "extra," or do they contribute to whatever the content is?

> When the author and illustrator are not the same person, which one answers the questions suggested above, and what if the answers are not the same?

Patricia Cianciolo provides a thorough and stimulating discussion of these and other issues. She believes that illustrations in childrens books are significant, both as art forms and as important facets of literature.

The author presents a most detailed description of widely used techniques and media. If the reader is unfamiliar with gouache, linocut, or painterly he will learn what these terms mean, and which illustrators have used them to good advantage.

The reader will recall that a major objective of this series is to acquaint teachers and prospective teachers with some effective techniques for using literature with children. In her chapter, "Using Illustrations in the School," the author begins with the promise that "illustrated books are much preferred by children." She notes that illustrated books are not appropriate for preschoolers and primary age youngsters alone: "The youngest as well as the oldest child can gain considerable fun and pleasure from reading an attractively illustrated and well-written book."

The reader should, after completing this book, have much more insight into the illustrator's craft and the contributions illustrations make to books for children; and he should be able to look at, to perceive, the art which is an integral part of most excellent children's books with a deeper appreciation. He should, also, be better equipped to share some of these ideas and feelings with children, so that they, too, may read and look with more pleasure and much more understanding.

Pose Lamb, Editor

preface

Examination of children's books that have been published in recent years will reveal that these books are illustrated with pictures that vary widely in style and in artistic quality. Many of the books are illustrated by most competent graphic artists who have mastered aspects of design and the handling of media. They illustrate the action and plot clearly with pictures that are imaginative and beautiful. Unfortunately, however, some recent publications are illustrated by less talented artists.

Illustrations can contribute much to help children grow in their interest in reading and in their appreciation of fine books. This is likely to be the case if the book illustrations interpret and extend the story in an artistic manner and in a style that is suitable to the young reading audience. Hopefully, this book will help bring the children and the well-illustrated books together.

It is intended that the various facts about the illustrations in children's books which the writer has included in this manuscript will help the student of children's literature (be he an elementary school teacher, a school librarian, or an undergraduate student in a teacher education program) become familiar with the varieties of illustrated books that are available for children; to acquire the rudiments of information about the styles of art in the pictures that contemporary artists use in their illustrations; to appreciate the impact that the artist's media have on his creations; and to acquire some insight into the methods that can be used to create in children a keener awareness and an attitude of critical evaluation of the illustrations in the stories that they read. It is hoped that the readers of this book will be led to discover and to appreciate new and better illustrated children's literature so that their young pupils can be helped to find joy in good books and to develop a love for them.

P.C.

chapter 1

appraising illustrations in children's books

There are large numbers of children's books published each year, and most of these books have illustrations in them. Devotees of the more traditional and classic art forms are likely to react negatively to the unconventional illustrations that appear in many of the currently published children's books. Some book evaluators claim the illustrations are too realistic; others claim the illustrations are too imaginative, decorative, or abstract. There is little agreement. One can only say that appraisal of the art in these books should be in terms of the needs of today's children, and today's children have many and varied needs. The young modern is likely to be appreciative and accepting of pictures done in contemporary and conservative art styles. Still, he needs many of the beautiful books done in both the new and the traditional art if he is to recognize the beauty of each.

Whether the illustrations are made by the author himself or by a book artist, the function of the illustrator is to use the graphic art form to help tell the significant aspects of the story and to extend the text. This rule applies to the picture book where author and artist share almost equally the responsibility for telling the story. It also applies to the illustrated novel which has only a few pictures.

Types of Illustrated Books

There are extremes in the ways in which illustrations are used in books. There are children's books which consist only of pictures and have no text at all. In *The Magic Stick*, written and illustrated by Kjell Ringi, the illustrations carry the complete load in the way of literary connotation. This book without words would delight children three to six years of age. Balancing line drawings with vibrant three-color pictures, *The Magic Stick* reveals the magic that children can find in ordinary

Illustration for THE MAGIC
STICK, written and illustrated
by Kjell Ringi. Copyright ©
1968 by Kjell Sorensen-Ringi.
Reprinted with permission of
Harper & Row, Publishers.

things. With fine humor and invention, Mr. Ringi permits the imaginative reader to become a pirate with a telescope, a weight lifter, and
a general leading a parade. *The Magic Stick* is the ultimate example of
a book that shows that pictures can speak in many languages, that there
is a universality in the language of illustrations.

Another book in which the illustrations carry the load in the way
of literary connotation is *One, Two, Where's My Shoe?* by Tomi Ungerer.
This is a gay pictorial search for a little boy's shoe, and shoes can be
found in the most unlikely places. The dog's snout is really a shoe! So
are the bodies of the birds in flight, the man's torso, the ship's hull, the
alligator's body, the Egyptian's mustache, the fish's mouth, the cannon's
barrel, and so on. The illustrations are simple line drawings done in cartoon style. They harmonize nicely with the witty game of hide-and-seek—
as Tomi Ungerer views it.

Contrasted with the books which consist primarily of pictures are
those which contain marginal drawings that decorate the pages and do
not have the slightest connection with the accompanying text. These
pictures are not book illustrations in the truest sense, however. The
pictures that accompanied the chapbooks, so popular during the eighteenth century, served primarily to decorate these books. They did not
illustrate them in the proper meaning of the word.

A superficial examination of the illustrations that appear in *The Bat Poet,* which was written by Randall Jarrell, would lead one to say that this book belongs in this category. Not so. Maurice Sendak's illustrations are imaginative and decorative, but they do rest upon the text. They are in themselves an extension of the text, because each says things visually that were not said in words. The illustrations do indeed elucidate the story of a little brown bat who cannot sleep during the day and who makes up perceptive poems about the owl, the mocking bird, the chipmunk, and his own bat boyhood. In a very sophisticated manner, Sendak's pen drawings extend the text and masterfully depict the mood, the tones, and the overtones of this lovable fable. *The Bat Poet* was among the ninety-six titles that were shown in the American Institute of Graphic Arts Children's Book Show in 1965.

The story, the pictures, and the graphic presentation are all one when the worth of an illustrated book is being evaluated. So far as the pictures are concerned, it is not the amount of illustration that matters. It is how the pictures complete and integrate with the story. The illustrator has an artistic responsibility to concern himself with the *significance* of the story when he prepares the pictures. This is exactly what Sendak has accomplished in the total design of *The Bat Poet* and with the relatively few illustrations he made for it. This type of book is properly termed an illustrated book to differentiate it from a picture book.

But there is another kind of illustrated book. This is the one with a longer text and a more complex plot than is generally available to the pre-school child. There are numerous pictures included in this second type of illustrated book. But in proportion to the length of the text and the number of situations and characters included in the main plot and subplots, there are fewer illustrations than there usually are in the picture books for the very young reader. Books that are of this type demand a longer attention span, for the story takes longer to read.

An example of this second type of illustrated book is *The Jazz Man* by Mary Hays Weik which is illustrated with numerous superb woodcuts made by Ann Grifalconi. Both text and pictures express a Negro family's struggle for understanding and love. It is a story for readers from ages nine through twelve. The story of Zeke, a crippled boy living in Harlem; his parents' love for him; the family's experience of finding moments of happiness in hearing the jazz played by their neighbor and his friends; the reality of the cold, hunger, and lonliness realized by Zeke when his mother and dad leave him are some of the aspects depicted by Mary Hays Weik and Ann Grifalconi in this well-written and uniquely-illustrated book. This moving story could not be told as effectively by way of an abbreviated text or fewer illustrations. Nor is it one that would be fully appreciated or even understood, for that matter, by an immature child. *The Jazz Man* is a fine picture book for an older, mature child. It is perfect proof that profusely-illustrated books can be appealing to children in the age range that, wrongly, we tend to assume has long since outgrown them. *The Jazz Man* was a runner-up for the 1967 Newbery Award, a medal awarded annually to the author of an original, creative work that is considered a distinguished contribution to American literature for children. There is little question about Mary Weik's writing in *The Jazz Man,* for it is exquisite, but Ann Grifalconi's illustrations are unquestionably an essential part of this book.

Picture Books Described. The picture book is simply a special form of an illustrated book. Traditionally, educators and publishers do have some specific elements in mind when they speak of a picture book. Typically, the picture book is addressed primarily to the young child. The picture book usually contains a simple plot developed by way of a brief text which the youngster enjoys having read to him, and numerous pictures which enable him to comprehend the story independently of the text. Hopefully, the text is an important part of the book and worthy of the pictures that accompany it. The text alone is not the "heart" of the story and neither are the illustrations. The two must be together.

Any number of titles exemplifies well this type of picture book. Those created by Ezra Jack Keats and Robert McCloskey, although the styles of the texts and illustrations in each differ markedly, are the sort that properly fit this type of illustrated book. In their books, there is thorough fusion of pictures and words. Both the stories and the illustrations in the books created by these author-artists are typified by a creative artistic expression which serves to extend the reader's experiences, experiences which are intended, hopefully, to heighten the child's awareness of the world about him and help him gain a more complete understanding of self. Included in this type of picture book are Taro Yashima's *Crow Boy,* John Schoenherr's *The Barn,* and Leo Lionni's *The Biggest House in the World.* Also included in this type of picture book are those in which the alphabet, the numbers, Mother Goose rhymes, and other poems are pictorially depicted. The Mother Goose books done by Rojankovsky, Celestino Piatti and Tasha Tudor fall into this category of picture books, as do the number books by Ed Emberley and Brian Wildsmith.

It is for this kind of illustrated book—the picture book—that the Caldecott Medal is awarded each year. This annual award, a medal, is presented by the Children's Services Division of the American Library Association to the artist who has created the most distinguished picture book of the year. The award is in honor of Randolph J. Caldecott, the nineteenth century English illustrator of books for children. In order to be eligible for the Caldecott Medal, books must meet the following terms: the text must be worthy of the book but need not be the work of the artist; the pictures rather than the text are the most important part of the book; there are no limitations as to the age level of the intended reading audience of the picture book but traditionally, the Caldecott Medal has been awarded for the art work in the books that are addressed to young children; the artist must be a citizen or resident of the United States; and the book must have been published in the United States during the year preceding the presentation of the award.

Illustrations for Young Readers

Both the text and the illustrations in an illustrated book are important. Each is a unique creative accomplishment; together picture and word must blend so well that it will seem as if one person had been responsible for both.

It is not particularly unusual for an author to illustrate his own story; examples abound of illustrators who have experienced considerable success in creating the pictures for their own books. Beatrix Potter included her own exquisitely detailed, pastel-tinted illustrations in her tales about Peter Rabbit, Jemima Puddle-Duck, Tom Kitten, Squirrel Nutkin, and Benjamin Bunny, to name only a few of her delightful creatures. Ludwig Bemelmans wrote the five widely known *Madeline* books and made gay, colorful expressionistic-styled pictures for them, using water color as his media. His illustrations give the impression that he lost no time with details in drawing, but close examination will reveal that details are there. Robert McCloskey wrote quite a number of picture books. The Caldecott Medal Award winners, *Time of Wonder* and *Make Way for Ducklings,* were his own stories, illustrated by him in his inimitably humorous and gently satirical fashion. He has used varied media to make the pictures for his books, but watercolor was used for *Time of Wonder,* and lithographic pencil on grained zinc was used for *Make Way for Ducklings.* Most often, however, artists choose to make pictures that illustrate stories created by someone other than himself.

Something of Significance is Said. Picture books have long been among the first steps in a child's learning. They have served as an illustrated informant and guide to the world about him. Picture books have introduced new ideas to the reader. Concepts gained previously are often reinforced or extended by the illustrated book. Children have the intellectual capacity and they have the imaginative powers to enjoy picture books that express a variety of ideas and concepts, but the pictures and text must portray ideas and concepts that are within the realm of the readers' understanding and interest. The reader of *Wildfire,* for example, would probably have to be within the age range of eight through twelve years to appreciate fully the text and pictures that tell the important story of a small flame that secretly kindles a gigantic fire. The poetic prose, written by Evans G. Valens, Jr., and the effective, exquisite pictures done by Clement Hurd, typify this book. Yet neither the story nor the illustrations would impress the immature or inexperienced reader to any significant extent. On the other hand, the very young child would be delighted by the text and the pictures of Maurice Sendak's *Where the Wild Things Are,* and Ezra Jack Keats' *Peter's Chair.* The fantasy in the one and the reality in the other are of the type a young reader can imagine or else has already experienced. The original and imaginative pictures and brief text of *Where the Wild Things Are* portray a story about a little boy's adventure with fanciful monsters, a story that would thoroughly thrill children within the three to five years age range. The illustrations in this book depict a roguish little boy and big, ludicrous beasts to stir the creative imaginations of young readers. They are done in dark green and blue tempera contrasted with shades of purple. Pen and ink crosshatching strokes are used effectively to achieve texture and shading. Different from *Where the Wild Things Are,* but still of interest to readers in the same age range, is *Peter's Chair,* which conveys a young boy's reaction to having to play more quietly than has been his habit, and to having to give up to his baby sister the belongings he has outgrown. Keats uses collage and pen-and-ink with skill.

The story and the illustrations that make up a picture book will be appreciated and enjoyed by the reader if the contents have significance to him, if they have integrity, and if they extend his experience and heighten his awareness of the world around him. All of the books mentioned above can accomplish these very things when they are given to the right child at the right time. But a child's interests are infinite, and he has a fondness for a world that is filled with the tiniest of details, as well as one that is filled with the biggest of forms. Thus, he must be given illustrated books that will cause him to look for and see many things. He needs books that will lead him toward many imaginative adventures. Most young people enjoy picture books about serious as well as humorous things, and so would probably like the ones that are discussed below.

The gay and fun-filled picture story entitled *An Anteater Named Arthur* by Bernard Waber is illustrated with charming cartoon-styled drawings done with felt-tipped pens and Magic Markers. The young reader will find much of himself in Arthur who is described as being "helpful, understanding, well-behaved, sensible, orderly, and responsible; yet messy, argumentative, forgetful, finicky, indecisive, and irresponsible."

This same reader would also very likely enjoy the serious and touching story of *Salt Boy* by Mary Perrine. This picture book, illustrated by Leonard Weisgard, tells the story of a Navajo Indian boy's harrowing experience as he is forced to lasso a lamb swept away in a flash flood.

The young reader wants stories about ordinary things as well as the very unique. And so he would probably appreciate McCloskey's *One Morning in Maine*. Great satisfaction may be experienced upon introduction to the characters of *One Morning in Maine*. Both text and illustrations realistically tell of a child's reaction to losing her first tooth. It is a story that brings joy and excitement to every-day living and to just growing up.

The Burning Rice Fields, by Sara Cone Bryant, and illustrated in pastels by Mamoru Funai, or Margaret Hodges' *The Wave,* illustrated with cardboard cuts and color overlays by Blair Lent, are two versions of a Japanese legend which portray a unique situation in which an old man burns the rice fields in order to bring the people away from the shore village that is about to be engulfed by a tidal wave.

Our young reader enjoys books about the real as well as the imaginary. A very real situation is described in *Evan's Corner* by Elizabeth Starr Hill. The text and Nancy Grossman's illustrations, which are done in soft watercolors, portray a vivid and sympathetic story of a little boy who lives in a two-room Harlem apartment with his big family. He is given a corner in which he can be "lonely" in his own way.

Contrasted with this story of reality is the modern, fanciful tale entitled *The Country Bunny and the Little Gold Shoes,* by DuBose Heyward, an interesting account telling how the Easter Rabbits are chosen and how Easter eggs are delivered. The matter-of-fact illustrations by Marjorie Flack make this charming fantasy even more believable.

Each of the aforementioned books varies in content, in writing style, and in the type of illustrations. The contents of the text and illustrations in each book will help the child to envision his two worlds—the real and the imaginary, the actual and the ideal, in a new and vital way.

Audience Is Understood and Respected. If the book is addressed to children, the book artist must have a feeling for children as people. He must be aware of, and have respect for, their likes and dislikes. This quality of keen sensitivity to what children are like, and also to what they like, is apparent in *One Morning in Maine*—or in any of McCloskey's books, for that matter. In this picture book, the story line and the beautiful dark blue, double-page spreads enable the child to read about things that are important to him. In a genial satirical manner such meaningful realities of childhood as the following are considered: one must learn how to squeeze toothpaste onto the toothbrush; one must realize that a loose tooth means that one is growing up; and one must consider the fact that the vanilla ice cream cone (as opposed to a chocolate one) should be given to a little sister "so the drips won't spot."

The book artist must be aware of children's capacity to understand and to make judgments about the story and its accompanying pictures. He needs to know when and in what way children's tastes differ from adults' tastes. For example, there are few children within the age range which usually enjoys the Mother Goose rhymes who could appreciate the off-beat humor depicted in the illustrations that fill *The Chas. Addams Mother Goose.* However, there is little doubt that this oversized, colorful picture book would be enjoyed by the sophisticated teen-ager and adult. Conversely, *The Tall Book of Mother Goose* by Feodor Rojankovsky interprets the rhymes as most modern younger children would imagine them. Rojankovsky's characters are natural looking youngsters dressed in

Illustration for THE CHAS. ADDAMS MOTHER GOOSE, written and illustrated by Charles Addams. Copyright © 1967 by Charles Addams. Reprinted with permission of Harper & Row, Publishers.

contemporary clothes, and the animals are delightfully appealing and expressive.

The integrity of the young reader must not be violated by an interpretation that is coy or condescending. Instead, the artists must radiate a rich human warmth and a depth of emotion. The charming, unpretentious picture book by Ezra Jack Keats, entitled *The Snowy Day*, is worthy of mention in this respect. The colorful pictures done in collage and paint, and the simply-written, brief text constitute an appealing and youthful portrayal of a little boy's pleasure on a snowy day. The youngster joyfully crunches in the snow, makes tracks with his feet and stick, makes a snowman and snowballs, and makes angels in the snow. An artist such as Keats knows (as must any book artist) how to use his artistic talents to reach and challenge young readers. He knows how to use his talents to help his readers relax and enjoy their illustrated books.

Artistic Talent Prevails. Only really good illustrations can bring the conceptions of an author to completion. They should not merely decorate the book. Nor should they be merely a compilation of independent pictures in which the artist's only concern is to have *his* say. Ideally, there is a harmonious combination of textual and pictorial elements in any book that includes illustrations. Each component is significant and, in a picture book, each is of relatively equal importance. Admittedly, the story idea in any book must come first. This rule is applicable to the picture book, too.

When creating pictures he intends to use to illustrate a story, the artist's role is to make pictures that have storytelling qualities. He has to reveal in visual form the characters and setting of the story. This is especially important for the young child who "reads" the story through the pictures. An effective picture must be made out of each page. Each page must reveal action; each must be a change of scene. When one looks through a picture book, one should have the feeling that he is sitting through a theatrical spectacle.

In his acceptance speech when he was awarded the Caldecott Medal for his illustrations in *May I Bring A Friend?* by Beatrice Schenk de Regniers, Beni Montresor compared his vocation as costume and set designer for operas, ballets, and musical theatre with his work as a children's book artist. He said, "For me there is no difference between these two things—in the methods, in the aims, or in the results. The blank page is like an empty stage that must be filled with scenes, costumes, movement, and theatrical crescendo. And the words and colors become the music."[1] His stage is called a picture book.

---

[1] Beni Montresor. "Caldecott Award acceptance," *The Horn Book Magazine.* 41:370 (August, 1965).

Picture copyright © 1964 by Beni Montresor. From MAY I BRING A FRIEND? by Beatrice Schenk de Regniers. Used with permission of Atheneum Publishers.

A whole succession of pictures in a book must make an effective, clear, and simple design that will get the reader's attention and set the mood of the story. This was done aptly in Janice Udry's *The Moon Jumpers*, in which Maurice Sendak's luminous illustrations capture the joyous feeling of four children dancing in their bare feet in the moonlight of a quiet summer evening. The illustrations in this stunning book, which was a runner-up for the Caldecott Medal, are done in full color.

One might ask at this point, "Will children appreciate and grasp the meaning of a well-designed book?" Children crave something that is inspired and attractive. Nonetheless, they will take whatever is at hand. Good taste can be acquired, and if children are to get on the path that will lead them to recognize beautiful things, they must be given those things that are well-designed and pleasing to look at and that will enrich their lives. Handsome books must be placed within their sight and reach, and then they must be encouraged subtly and gently to read these books. A child can develop an appreciation of beauty through his handling of well-illustrated books. One need not settle for the lifeless illustrations that crowd the pages of many children's books, when quantities of beautiful and vital ones are available at libraries and book stores merely for the asking. It is not expecting too much that the books published for children of all ages should include drawings that are made by the greatest artists. It is never too early to give a young child books that are illustrated with the best and most substantial pictures so that his inborn tendencies to be imaginative and curious do not dwindle into dormancy or that his creative spirit become stunted by lack of nourishment.

Illustrations Go Beyond the Text. Book illustrations should constitute a work of decoration and should reflect a well-planned design. But they must accomplish still more than this. Whether the artist is making pictures for a picture book or for a book which is to contain only a few illustrations, he must help the reader to understand and visualize the text, to recreate the significant scenes and ideas from the story. The illustrations must be the equivalent of each significant emotion and thought expressed in the text.

There are only about seven illustrations in Barbara C. Smucker's story, *Wigwam in the City,* yet the superb woodcut prints of the artist,

Woodcuts by Gil Miret from the book WIGWAM IN THE CITY by Barbara C. Smucker. Copyright © 1966 by Barbara C. Smucker. Reproduced with permission of E. P. Dutton & Co., Inc.

Gil Miret, depict so well the experiences and the emotions of Susan Bearskin and her family when they leave their reservation home, Lac du Flambeau, in Wisconsin, and move to Chicago. These few illustrations do indeed have relevance to the text, but they accomplish much more than merely help the reader to interpret the text. Gil Miret, as should any accomplished book artist, created illustrations that do more than serve as a neutral vehicle for transmitting the text of the story. The illustrations encourage the reader to exercise his own imagination and go beyond the text. This is an essential and admirable goal of the book artist, for the awakening and strengthening of the imagination is one of the chief factors in the development of a child's mind.

Frequently, the artist is called upon to create illustrations that will cause the reader to enlarge on the story elements that were only hinted at in the text. In order to do this, the artist must offer a sufficient number of pictures with enough detail in each so that the reader can use them as a guide to extending the text and recalling the story. Once he has heard the story, the young reader should be able to retell it by studying the details in the pictures.

Beatrix Potter, who seems to have been a natural book illustrator, created what some authorities consider to be almost perfect picture books. She expressed herself freely in her drawings and her brief texts. Miss Potter's books have a colored picture on every spread, and on each page the text is limited to concise, simple sentences. Stories and pictures in *The Tale of Peter Rabbit* and *The Tale of Jemima Puddle-Duck*, as well as in her other tales of creatures of the farm and field are evidence of her sense of beauty, of her imaginative approach, and of her feelings for the countryside she loved.

There are innumerable other good illustrators of children's picture books. Certain graphic designers whose names quickly come to mind, because their illustrations carry far more detail and more substance than appears in the text, have brought fresh life to children's books over the last few years. For example, one artist who comes to mind is Celestino Piatti, widely known in Switzerland as an outstanding graphic designer, who authored and illustrated *The Happy Owls*. His work has the essential quality of communication and is brilliantly decorative as well. In his designs, the white paper is as important as the flat, colored poster illustrations.

Leo Lionni, an Amsterdam-born American, is another graphic designer who devotes much time and effort to finding new methods of visual communication. A talented painter and graphic designer, Lionni has created several stunning picture books. Two of his most widely acclaimed books are *Inch by Inch* and *The Biggest House in the World*. Each book has a rather brief text. Each is illustrated with original and imaginative, beautifully colored pictures. *Inch by Inch* is done in rice paper collage. The pages of *The Biggest House in the World* are filled with dramatic paintings, bold in design, rich in color.

There are the sumptuous, gloriously colored works of Alois Carigiet, a Swiss artist, who illustrated *A Bell for Ursli* and *The Snowstorm,* both of which were written by Selina Chonz. Carigiet's paintings are large, are done in full radiant color, and are filled with alluring detail. His books have the appearance of the classic picture book, and yet Carigiet's art is exquisitely modern. He was awarded a Hans Christian Andersen International Children's Book Medal in 1966.

Among the most productive and successful of the contemporary illustrators are Alice and Martin Provensen. Their drawings in *The Charge of the Light Brigade* are comparable to an early illumination or a Mogul painting. This picture book is a stunning graphic interpretation of Tennyson's poem. The double spread paintings are among the most beautiful and most dramatic pieces of illustration to appear in recent years and should be considered a significant contribution to book art.

Color and Shading May Be a Goal. Plenty of rich, harmonious color has been an important goal in children's literature. Color can be one way to attract children's attention to a book. More important, perhaps, is the fact that a major aim of color is to serve an expressive rather than a representational color-sense. According to some art critics, absolute imitation of color can scarcely be called art for it expresses so little of the human mind.

Examination of the colored illustrations that are included in children's books will reveal that few of the contemporary book artists and lithographers do try to present a sketch of a subject as it *really* is. Even the representational artists seem to go to great length to avoid the imitation of nature. Most book artists use tones and shades of color to express form as they see it, not as an attempt to imitate that form. Thus, the artist should be encouraged to use color freely.

If one agrees with this attitude toward color, he will ignore the associations of color, and he will not feel the need to copy the color of an object literally in order to aid realism. Free use of color will permit the artist (and the reader of a text illustrated with colored illustrations) to express his own feelings and emotions toward the subject.

It is extremely difficult to be objective when evaluating the book artist's use of color. Perusal of some of the critical reviews of children's picture books will reveal that by no means is there agreement among graphic artists or authorities in children's literature as to color harmony or "suitable" colors for children's books. There is very little agreement as to whether or not the colors used in any one book have helped to tell the author's message clearly. Each book reviewer will have a different opinion as to what he sees in the illustrations—or in the story, for that matter. For instance, one critic may feel that the colors Jacob Lawrence has used in *Harriet and the Promised Land* are "out of harmony" and unsuitable for children. Another will find the contrasting color combinations bold and angry, but completely appropriate for the author's message and for the audience to whom this moving narrative verse is addressed. Likewise, one may find that the colors used in Edward Lear and Ogden Nash's *The Scroobious Pip* are in delightful unity with the text. He may welcome the subtle distinctions between the warm and cool shades that Nancy Ekholm Burkert has used. Another reviewer may find that the combination of shades of colors used in *The Scroobious Pip* are too quiet, much too subtle to move the young reader.

In an article in which she reviewed the AIGA Children's Book Show that opened at the New York Public Library on March 6, 1961, Edna Beilenson stated that such color combinations of cerise, yellow, and clear blue against a background of black and white, or shades of blue green and violet, are not suitable to young children. Indeed, they are much more suitable, says Mrs. Beilenson, for a new perfume by Chanel, or for a gown by Schiaparelli or Oleg Cassini.[2]

Acceptance or rejection of Mrs. Beilenson's comment about colors "appropriate" for young children will depend largely upon personal opinion. One might bear in mind that a child is a product of his times, and that today these color combinations are considered by some art educators to be appropriate for children as well as for adults. Furthermore, each artist brings his unique perceptions to a story. His interpretations and the colors he finds appropriate to express his thoughts and feelings about the subject will, and should, differ from those of another artist. This individuality should be respected.

Brian Wildsmith makes exquisite use of brilliant colors. His works, painted in gouache, are usually in full color, and his style is representational with abstract tendencies. For example, in *Brian Wildsmith's 1, 2, 3's*, the numbers one through ten are illustrated with simple basic forms of the rectangle, the triangle, and the circle. His books employ a splendor of color combining most beautifully and effectively, clear and bright shades of orange, blue, black, chartreuse, fuchsia, purple, and yellow. Today's young moderns thoroughly enjoy these combinations despite the opinions of some graphic art critics.

Jacob Lawrence has used brilliant shades of poster paint to create a stunning book, *Harriet and the Promised Land*. This is a story in verse telling how Harriet Tubman, born a slave, escaped to the north and

---

[2]Edna Beilenson, "The AIGA Children's Book Show," *Publisher's Weekly* 180. 69-72 (March 6, 1961).

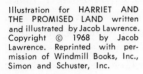
Illustration for HARRIET AND THE PROMISED LAND written and illustrated by Jacob Lawrence. Copyright © 1968 by Jacob Lawrence. Reprinted with permission of Windmill Books, Inc., Simon and Schuster, Inc.

freedom only to return nineteen times to lead more than three hundred of her people to freedom. In this large picture book, the artist has used flat yellow, red, black, brown, and blue in his stylized drawings. The exaggerated features of the characters are most expressionistic, as are the distortions of size and perspective. On each page, white space surrounds the picture and the brief text. Each page unto itself is an impressive picture, and yet each is a unified part of the book. Not everyone will like this book. In fact, some will find the illustrations (and the message of the text) discomfiting and "unpretty." The author-illustrator did not intend to have this picture book serve as a vehicle only to entertain little children. He wanted the reader of this book to feel and to empathize with the plight of Harriet Tubman and her people. The choice of color, the style of illustrating, and the brief and understated poetic text serve to provide a choice example of a truly expressionistic work of art.

Contrasting the use of brilliant color found in Wildsmith's and Lawrence's books are the soft, soothing colors found in *The Scroobious Pip*, illustrated by Nancy Ekholm Burkert, and mentioned previously. Mrs. Burkert's exquisite brush and ink drawings, which would also appeal to young readers, delineate the teeming forms of life celebrated in the rhythmic poem in which all the animals in the world gather around a strange inscrutable creature that is part bird, part beast, part insect, and part fish. The drawings are representational, with emphasis on craftsmanship and particularization. Mrs. Burkert's concept of Pip is based on Edward Lear's own small pen drawings that were included in his incomplete manuscript which is now available in Harvard University's Houghton Library in Cambridge, Massachusetts.[3]

All three of these artists, Lawrence, Wildsmith, and Burkert, make wide use of marvelous color combinations, and the writer does think they are suitable for children growing up in today's world. None of the artists referred to overstrains the use of color; nor does he use it as superficial decoration. Admittedly, there are some children's books which contain paintings in heavy garish colors. Some contain illustrations that are done in painting techniques that overwhelm the narrative they are supposed to depict. But quantities of beautiful books are available and should be read to children and examined by them.

Children enjoy books illustrated in monochrome (in one color and white), if the figures stand out enough and express action and vitality. There are several picture books done in monochrome, for example, *The Biggest Bear* by Lynd Ward or *Picture Bible* by Felix Hoffmann. Robert McCloskey's Caldecott Medal book, *Make Way for Ducklings,* in monochromatic (sepia) and his delightful story, *One Morning in Maine,* is done in blue and white. A tense drama in animal life, the compelling story of a skunk and an owl's struggle for survival, is told in John Schoenherr's *The Barn,* with text and black and white pictures. These artists do not depend upon color to state their messages. Instead, they make use of shading to suggest light and dark and color. The illustrations in each of the books cited above are good and are fully enjoyed and appreciated by children who see them.

Sizes and Shapes Should Vary. The contents of the illustrated books for children vary, as do the style of writing and the illustrations. It is desirable, also, that there be considerable variation in the sizes and shapes of the books that are made available to the young reader. Children delight in handling the very big, the tiny, the thick, the square, the rectangular, and the tall picture books. Oftentimes, the very shape of the book adds more credibility to the story line. The size and shape of the book can also emphasize the mood of the story or can make the setting more explicit and believable.

Included in a good picture book collection would be books such as the following: Feodor Rojankovsky's *The Tall Book of Mother Goose,* a tall and slim book. The characters in these beloved rhymes are natural-looking and appealing. *The Book of Nursery and Mother Goose Rhymes*

---

[3]Edward Lear and Ogden Nash. *The Scroobious Pip.* Illustrated by Nancy Ekholm Burkert. (New York: Harper & Row, Publishers, 1968), Foreword.

by Marguerite de Angeli is just the opposite of Rojankovsky's book. It is thick and broad and contains numerous full-page illustrations painted in soft pastels. The characters are beautiful, delicate creatures. Maurice Sendak's *Nutshell Library* is a package of four wonderfully humorous

Illustration for "Alligators All Around" from NUT-SHELL LIBRARY, written and illustrated by Maurice Sendak. Copyright © 1962 by Maurice Sendak. Reprinted with permission of Harper & Row, publishers.

books. Measuring only 3 3/4 inches, each little book offers much to the young reader. Illustrated with pen drawings in Sendak's wonderful cartoon style, the books interpret the months of the year, the alphabet, the numbers from one through ten, and a cautionary tale. Captivating picture books by Beatrix Potter such as *The Tale of Jemima Puddle-Duck* or *The Tale of Peter Rabbit* which contain full-color spreads and are only an inch or so bigger than the four volumes of the *Nutshell Library* are also a *must* in a picture book collection. Another *must* is the big rectangular book by Isaac Bashevis Singer entitled *Mazel and Shlimazel; or The Milk of a Lioness,* which contains strong, heavily-lined, colored illustrations by Margot Zemach. Pictures in this book effectively underlie the humor and the tradition quality of this Yiddish folktale.

Other Considerations. Writers of good children's books do not depend entirely upon help from the graphic artists, for literature has its own forms of expression. Whether or not illustrations accompany the text, the language in the text must create its own conceptions. When illustrations are used, the artist may not impose his conceptions of the story with definitiveness or precise literalness, for this would "interfere in a very unpleasant way with the readers' own dreams."[4] The illustrations must be created in a manner that permits the reader to be completely free to use his own creative and imaginative powers when interpreting the words and the pictures.

A succession of flashy, experimental, or unusual pictures in a book may very well attract a child's attention, but the attention of the reader will not be held long by the illustrations alone. The story that is told by both the text and the illustrations must be a good one. It may be long or short, but it must be a story that is of interest to the reader. The language used to tell the story must be rich in imagery. It must be void of clichés, and it must encourage the reader to sense, in his own youthful way, the composition, the perspective, and the use of color in the illustrations. Janice Udry's *The Moon Jumpers* is an excursion into the beautiful world of quality literature and genuine art, an expression of beauty which should be in every illustrated book, for beautiful expression denotes quality.

Beautiful expression can be found in other illustrated stories, too, but in each case, the stories must be told with language that is precise, colorful, and descriptive. Seldom is beauty of expression found in a book in which the vocabulary is controlled, for then the writer is too restricted to create a beautiful story. The vocabulary control does not permit him the freedom and range necessary for imaginative creative writing.

Wingfin and Topple, a large, handsome picture book, is written in exquisite poetic form by Evans G. Valens, Jr., and is illustrated by Clement Hurd with linoleum block prints on the grain of weathered wood. Both text and illustrations create fascinating images that capture the beauty and vastness of the sea, sky, and water. Both forms of artistic expression complement the other; each is made more beautiful by the presence of the other.

More factors than just the text and the illustrations are considered when appraising an illustrated book. There are several other important elements that can enhance the beauty of a volume and result in a fine illustrated book (as being distinguished from a book with fine illustrations). As we stated earlier, decisions must be made as to such aesthetic concerns as the shape and size of the book, whether the illustrations will be in color or in black and white, and the number of colors if the decision is made to have color illustrations. Type face that is compatible with the style and color illustrations must be selected, too. As a rule, these decisions are made by the artist, together with the art director and the editor

---

[4] Roger Duvoisin, "Children's Book Illustration: The Pleasure and Problems," *Top of the News.* 22:30, (November, 1965).

of the publishing company. This is the team that must interpret the story and produce a book which will be of interest to young readers, a book which they can read and look at with pleasure.

Summary. The illustrated book is defined as any book in which the text is accompanied by illustrations that are pertinent to the text. The picture book is a special form of an illustrated book. In the picture book, there is a thorough fusion of pictures and words.

Qualities which should characterize the illustrations in children's books have been cited. The contents of the story and the illustrations must have significance to the young reader. The illustrations should heighten and extend the reader's awareness of the world around him. They should lead him to an appreciation of beauty. The style and content of the illustrations should be child-like; that is, they should be neither coy nor condescending, nor should they be adult-like in the level of sophistication. The illustrations should have story-telling qualities so that such literary components as action, mood, theme, setting, and story-line are revealed. They should enlarge upon the story elements that were hinted at in the text and should include details that will awaken and strengthen the imagination of the reader and permit him to interpret the words and pictures in a manner that is unique to him.

Rich and harmonious color should be used to serve an expressive, rather than a representational, purpose. Monochrome and black and white illustrations are appropriate for use in children's books, too, if the shading and contrasts are used so that the figures stand out, so that action is expressed, and so that an adequate degree of warmth and vitality is reflected. Sizes and shapes of the illustrated books for children should vary, as should the style of writing and the styles of art that are used to tell and interpret the story.

SELECTED REFERENCES

ADDAMS, CHARLES. *The Chas. Addams Mother Goose.* New York: Harper & Row, Publishers, 1967.

ANDERSEN, HANS CHRISTIAN. *The Nightingale.* Translated by Eva LeGallienne. Illustrated by Nancy Ekholm Burkert. New York: Harper & Row, Publishers, 1965.

BEMELMANS, LUDWIG. *Madeline.* New York: The Viking Press, Inc., 1939.

BRYANT, SARA CONE. *The Burning Rice Fields.* Illustrated by Mamoru Funai. New York: Holt, Rinehart & Winston, Inc., 1963.

CHONZ, SELINA. *A Bell for Ursli.* Illustrated by Alois Carigiet. New York: Henry Z. Walck, Inc., 1950.

———. *The Snowstorm.* Illustrated by Alois Carigiet. New York: Henry Z. Walck, Inc., 1958.

DE ANGELI, MARGUERITE. *The Book of Nursery and Mother Goose Rhymes.* Garden City, New York: Doubleday & Company, Inc., 1954.

DE REGNIERS, BEATRICE SCHENK. *May I Bring a Friend?* Illustrated by Beni Montresor. New York: Atheneum Publishers, 1964.

HEYWARD, DuBOSE. *The Country Bunny and the Little Gold Shoes.* Illustrated by Marjorie Flack. Boston: Houghton Mifflin Company, 1939.

HILL, ELIZABETH STARR. *Evan's Corner.* Illustrated by Nancy Grossman. New York: Holt, Rinehart & Winston, Inc., 1967.

HODGES, MARGARET. *The Wave.* Illustrated by Blair Lent. Boston: Houghton Mifflin Company, 1964.

JARRELL, RANDALL. *The Bat Poet.* Illustrated by Maurice Sendak. New York: The Macmillan Company, 1964.

KEATS, EZRA JACK. *Peter's Chair.* New York: Harper & Row, Publishers, 1967.

———. *The Snowy Day.* New York: The Viking Press, Inc., 1962.

LAWRENCE, JACOB. *Harriet and the Promised Land.* New York: Windmill Books, Inc., Simon and Schuster, Inc., 1968.

LEAR, EDWARD and NASH, OGDEN. *The Scroobious Pip.* Illustrated by Nancy Ekholm Burkert. New York: Harper & Row, Publishers, 1968.

LIONNI, LEO. *The Biggest House in the World.* New York: Pantheon Books, Inc., 1968.

———. *Inch by Inch.* New York: Ivan Obolensky, Inc., 1960.

McCLOSKEY, ROBERT. *Make Way for Ducklings.* New York: The Viking Press, Inc., 1941.

———. *One Morning in Maine.* New York: The Viking Press, Inc., 1952.

———. *Time of Wonder.* New York: The Viking Press, Inc., 1957.

McNEER, MAY. *The American Indian Story.* Illustrated by Lynd Ward. New York: Farrar, Straus & Giroux, Inc., 1963.

PERRINE, MARY. *Salt Boy.* Illustrated by Leonard Weisgard. New York: Abelard-Schuman, Limited, 1968.

PIATTI, CELESTINO. *The Happy Owls.* New York: Atheneum Publishers, 1964.

POTTER, BEATRIX. *The Tale of Jemima Puddle-Duck.* New York: Frederick Warne & Co., Inc., 1908.

———. *The Tale of Peter Rabbit.* New York: Frederick Warne & Co., Inc., 1902.

RINGI, KJELL. *The Magic Stick.* New York: Harper & Row, Publishers, 1968.

ROJANKOVSKY, FEODOR. *The Tall Book of Mother Goose.* New York: Harper & Row, Publishers, 1942.

SASEK, MIROSLAV. *This is New York.* New York: The Macmillan Company, 1960.

———. *This is Paris.* New York: The Macmillan Company, 1959.

SCHOENHERR, JOHN. *The Barn.* Boston: Atlantic-Little, Brown and Company, 1968.

SENDAK, MAURICE. *Nutshell Library.* New York: Harper & Row, Publishers, 1962.

———.*Where the Wild Things Are.* New York: Harper & Row, Publishers, 1963.

SINGER, ISAAC BASHEVIS. *Mazel and Shlimazel; or The Milk of a Lioness.* Illustrated by Margot Zemach. New York: Farrar, Straus & Giroux, Inc., 1968.

SMALL, ERNEST. *Baba Yaga.* Illustrated by Blair Lent. Boston: Houghton Mifflin Company, 1966.

SMUCKER, BARBARA C. *Wigwam in the City.* Illustrated by Gil Miret. New York: E. P. Dutton & Co., Inc., 1966.

STEVENSON, ROBERT LOUIS. *A Child's Garden of Verses.* Illustrated by Brian Wildsmith. New York: Franklin Watts, Inc., 1966.

TENNYSON, ALFRED LORD. *The Charge of the Light Brigade*. Illustrated by Alice and Martin Provensen. New York: Golden Press, Inc., 1964.

TUDOR, TASHA. *Mother Goose*. New York: Henry Z. Walck, Inc., 1944.

UDRY, JANICE. *The Moon Jumpers*. Illustrated by Maurice Sendak. New York: Harper & Row, Publishers, 1959.

UNGERER, TOMI. *One, Two, Where's My Shoe?* New York: Harper & Row, Publishers, 1964.

VALENS, EVANS G., JR. *Wildfire*. Illustrated by Clement Hurd. Cleveland: The World Publishing Company, 1963.

———. *Wingfin and Topple*. Illustrated by Clement Hurd. Cleveland: The World Publishing Company, 1962.

WABER, BERNARD. *An Anteater Named Arthur*. Boston: Houghton Mifflin Company, 1967.

WARD, LYND. *The Biggest Bear*. Boston: Houghton Mifflin Company, 1952.

WEIK, MARY HAYS. *The Jazz Man*. Illustrated by Ann Grifalconi. New York: Atheneum Publishers, 1966.

WILDSMITH, BRIAN. *Brian Wildsmith's 1, 2, 3's*. New York: Franklin Watts, Inc., 1965.

YASHIMA, TARO. *Crow Boy*. New York: The Viking Press, Inc., 1955.

chapter 2

styles of art in children's books

Literature is an art form which has its own means of expression. The content as well as other narrative elements of literature provide the materials with which the graphic artist builds an attractive page and gives order and visual qualities to that page.[1] It is in the order, in the arrangement of line and color, that the style of art can be identified.

The art in our modern picture books must say something to children and must say it in a loose way so that the reader is free to bring his own interpretation to the writing and to the book illustrations. Uri Shulevitz, noted illustrator who has been cited by the Society of Illustrators and the American Institute of Graphic Arts, stated that he usually tries to suggest and evoke rather than state rigidly, so as to encourage the child to participate actively, filling in with his own imagination. Shulevitz emphasized that this approach is based on the belief that his audience is intelligent and active rather than passive.[2] Hopefully, too, the children's book artist will express his ideas in a manner that is so original and interesting to the reader that the book cannot be ignored.

Inventive book design and book illustration can be found in many of the children's books that have been published in recent years. Consider the emphatic typography and cheerful assortment of soft, bright colors for the wood engravings in Antonio Frasconi's *See Again, Say Again*. This delightful, inventive approach to book design extends an irresistible invitation to the young reading audience. Tasha Tudor's series, *A Is for Annabelle, I Is One,* and *Around the Year,* with their charmingly feminine pastel illustrations, are quickly recognized as books that would

---

[1]Roger Duvoisin "Children's Book Illustration: The Pleasure and Problems," *Top of the News.* 22:31 (November, 1965).

[2]Lee Kingman, Joanna Foster, and Ruth Giles Lontoft. "Uri Shulevitz." *Illustrators of Children's Books, 1957-1966.* (Boston: The Horn Book, Inc., 1968). p. 174.

be cherished by children the world over. The illustrative art in these books, as is in quantities of other children's books, is imaginative, dramatic, and expressive. The art in each book is typified by originality. It is an originality which is not at all superficial as so often happens when an artist is too conscious of making his illustrations "new," when his attention has been directed toward making the expression different rather than on the thoughts he was supposed to express. There is little room for the children's book artist who strives for novelty merely by being different, and who is giving vent to eccentricity through illustrating books. This would defeat the purpose of the book. A book is intended to be read, and the illustrations must legitimately help to deliver the writer's message.

It does not follow necessarily that the personality of the book artist is destroyed, or that he becomes a servant to the writer. The talented illustrator can still use his own creative powers. His personality can still be preserved through the spirit of the particular literary selection he is illustrating. Marcia Brown is an outstanding example of a contemporary artist who meets the requirements of each story that she illustrates, but manages to do so on her own terms. Each of her picture books is her very own personal creation despite the fact that many of them contain illustrations of well-known folktales. She uses vigorous crayon and gouache drawings to illustrate *The Three Billy Goats Gruff*, bold and graceful woodcut designs in *Once a Mouse,* and delicate drawings in pen line and colored crayon for *Cinderella*. In each book, Marcia Brown retains the mood and period of time peculiar to the traditional text, but she makes her own exquisite pictures, using different media and art styles for each story. The story-line and the illustrations for each book are undeniably compatible.

Style in illustrative art, like style in writing, is a rather elusive quality. It is influenced by the content and the mood of the story. It is also influenced by the age of the reader as well as the artist's concept of his audience. The younger the child, the more representational the art style should be. To some extent, the younger the child, the more conservative the artist will have to be in his use of space, in his use of the combinations and color relations, in the dramatic use of forms and lines, and in his treatment of surfaces. If the artist views children as being only sweet and angelic, if he tends to be condescending in his way with children, in all probability this will be revealed in the style of art used in his illustrations. On the contrary, if he respects his young audience, if he believes they have the maturity and intelligence necessary to appreciate and understand illustrations that are more impressionistic and sophisticated in nature, this will be evident in his illustrations.

There are other factors that influence an artist's style. Among these are interrelated factors such as the basic personality of the artist, his creative talent, the media he uses to make his pictures, and his mastery of the media and techniques employed.

We are in an era in which there is an astonishing wealth of creative talent involved in illustrating books for children. The artists are rapidly breaking away from tradition. Their book designs and styles reveal independent thinking and respect for experimentation. There is an ever-mounting number of artists who speak freely, who refuse to succumb to the pressures of popular taste. Book artists make use of unconventional and contemporary art work as well as of the more conventional.

The influence of the ideas of fine artists is readily recognized in today's styles of art used in children's book illustrations. In fact, practically every artistic style suggestive of famous artists such as Raoul Dufy, Wassily Kandinsky, Paul Klee, Marc Chagall, Paul Cézanne, Vincent Van Gogh, and others can be identified in the illustrations of many modern picture books.

All the graphic arts have profited from the discoveries that the painters made as they moved toward abstraction, although the pure abstract painter has never illustrated books. The abstractionist must completely eliminate the subject in conceiving his painting. Thus he cannot apply his art in book illustration.[3] Nonetheless, children's book artists have been influenced greatly by the evolution of painting toward abstraction. Their illustrations often hint at or use to varying degrees symbols, illusions, and imagery.

A catholicity of taste is often displayed in the pages of modern children's books. Numerous remarkable books can be found in which the modern book artists have assimilated the various art styles . . . representationalism, cubism, expressionism, impressionism, and the pointillist technique. No one school seems to predominate. Also, there is a strong movement toward combining folkloristic elements with a modern technique.

Folk artists tend to emphasize the modern view which makes use of agreeable rather than loud, artificial colors.

The wealth of shapes and sumptuous colors, the wonderfully original ideas and uninhibited experimentation in book design and art style, indicate how important children's book illustration currently is. This growing importance reveals to some extent, too, that much effort and creative ability is necessarily put forth in the making of good books

---

[3]Duvoisin, *Ibid.*, p. 30-31.

for children. Each of these books is a reminder that there is much beauty to see in children's literature, and fine books can permit children to experience pleasure from books at an early age.

It is indeed gratifying that one can find well-designed and well-decorated children's books. When beautiful books are placed constantly within their sight and reach, children are more likely to grow to recognize and prefer the things that are beautiful. They will be less likely to settle for the second-rate and lifeless illustrations which crowd the pages of some children's books. There will always be the mediocre books, the ones issued by publishers who do not seem to care what kind of market they find for their books, or who succumb to expediency for temporary profit. Hopefully, if a young child has read and examined books that are tastefully and beautifully illustrated, he will learn to enjoy distinctive art in paintings and in books. Some educators and artists maintain that a child unconsciously learns to appreciate fine art, that is, he learns very early in life to appreciate order, rhythm, and interesting arrangements of color from the picture books he sees. Marcia Brown has emphasized that if a child habitually sees well-designed pages in the picture books, the varied and interesting shapes may start a chain of reactions within him that could continue into adulthood. She maintains that the child's discrimination, along with whatever segments of his individuality he can manage to preserve, will be his main defense against the bombardment of visual materials that he is likely to face during most of his waking hours.[4]

An illustration can show us new ways of seeing; it can sharpen our perception; it can give us a deeper understanding of the relation between nature and man. Great art is more than a mere record of nature and what one sees. It is an expression of man's thoughts and feelings. However, a work of art must be more than expression of an artist's ideas and emotional responses. It must arouse in the viewer a kind of enjoyment that is long-lasting rather than one that is short-lived. Furthermore, a work of art must cause the viewer to stop and look, and then look again.

An artist's choice of style is a personal one. He needs a good eye for detail and a sensitivity to form. Regardless of the art style he uses to express his ideas and feelings, he needs a good memory for each of these. Artists of every age have interpreted reality in their own language of form and color. Since nature cannot be transcribed onto paper or canvas, it must be translated more simply by way of pictorial technique. Varied art styles have been originated by artists in their attempt to

---

[4]Marcia Brown. "Distinction in Picture Books," Illustrators of Children's Books; 1946-1956. Bertha Mahoney Miller et al. (Boston: Horn Book, Inc., 1958), pp. 6-10.

transmit their mental images and their feelings. In the pages that follow some of the art styles used by contemporary book artists are identified.

Representational Art. The power of the realist, or representational artist, lies in his ability to select from an object or an event exactly what is necessary to tell, only the important facts that typify that object or event, (but in a manner entirely different from that used by the photographer). The representational illustration is fairly decorative and transmits a feeling of formality and immediacy. It is concerned with the details and facts of the object itself. Outlines are exact and precise, as if one is viewing the scene closely. To a certain extent, there is a literalism and realism in a representational painting that controls the style, although a limited amount of distortion is permitted to emphasize the artist's message. Thus, a representational artist may speak freely with color and lines, and with round, smooth, undulating, and living curves. Modern representational artists oftentimes are more concerned with the anatomy and the details of their model than they are with its inner nature. Yet they are experimental enough so that their creative efforts are recognized as original works of art.

The realist stays rather close to the appearance of the objects, but it must be remembered that each of us has a different perception of a single object. Each of us will bring his own interpretation to a particular incident. The book artist, and everyone else, selects or abstracts thoughts from his experience (or from the written word) those features that are suitable, essential, and compatible to his purpose and personality.

The watercolor and pencil illustrations by Tasha Tudor are realistic in style, although they reveal the artist's nostalgic attitude toward nineteenth century Americana. In her beautiful and quaint alphabet book, *A Is for Annabelle,* Miss Tudor uses on old-fashioned, delicately illustrated doll. In *Becky's Birthday,* the story of a little farm girl of bygone years celebrating her tenth birthday, the artist-author depicts the happy events and surprises of the day in a realistic, and yet nostalgic manner, with charming and pleasing watercolor paintings, as well as with black and white pencil sketches. The wonderful candle-lighted, flower-bedecked birthday cake at the evening picnic party in the pasture by the river would bring pure delight to modern young readers.

Adrienne Adams, the creator of meticulously detailed scenes and attractive decorations for such books as Alice Goudey's *Butterfly Time,* and *Houses from the Sea,* and the Charles Scribner's Sons edition of Hans Christian Andersen's *Thumbelina,* captures living pictures of a child's world of reality and make-believe. She is a magnificent draftsman. Her concern for minute detail reveals as much, if not more, information than do the brief texts and stories she so often illustrates.

The handsome and vigorous representational lithograph prints made by Lynd Ward to illustrate his own *The Biggest Bear* and May McNeer's *The Canadian Story* depict animals and the woodlands in a manner that would delight any naturalist. The anatomical detail of the male Indians and of the galloping horses in May McNeer's *The American Indian Story* are particularly impressive. The bodies are muscular and sinewy. They

Illustration by Lynd Ward for THE AMERICAN INDIAN STORY by May McNeer. Copyright © 1963 by May McNeer and Lynd Ward. Reprinted with permission of Farrar, Straus & Giroux, Inc.

transmit a feeling of energy, so much so, that the reader feels a sympathetic tension in his own muscles. Ward's figures are creatures of almost perfect, normal proportions, with the one exception that his well-muscled figures are somewhat distorted about the chest, arms, and legs. It is this very distortion that accentuates the stunning rhythmic movements of the horse, for example, and the tremendous power and strength of the Indian. Lynd Ward's distortions serve only to highlight the authors' messages. He does not use distortions as a tool of caricatures to attract attention, to satirize, or to provide pure humor.

Expressionistic Art. Expressionism is diametrically opposed to imitational art. It is an expression of the artist's subjective emotion and

leans heavily toward abstraction. The essential or structural quality of
the object, as opposed to the outward aspects of the object, is a primary
concern of the expressionist. The artist's subjective emotional expression
about his reality (or object) is another, and perhaps major, concern.
Oftentimes, the first quick glance at an expressionist's painting will lead
one to equate it with the primitivism of children's art. Consider Ludwig
Bemelmans' work in the *Madeline* books. His sketches of the girls in the
private school, the long-robed nuns, the circus scenes, and the scenes
of Paris are typical of one type of expressionistic art and are rather childlike in nature. The influence of Paul Klee's and Raoul Dufy's styles of
expressionism can be recognized, although Bemelmans made the expressionistic style his own and applied it in his picture books.

There seems to be a close relationship between the work of Joseph
Low and Uri Shulevitz and that of Bemelmans. Low's sketches tend to
be bolder and heavier than Bemelmans', but both evidence a rather
whimsical tone in their sketches. The line drawings in Joseph Low's
Jack and the Beanstalk as told by Walter de la Mare, and the line drawings and brush tones in his own book entitled *The Big Cheese* match the
folk quality of each of these stories. Like Joseph Low, Uri Shulevitz,
talented illustrator of *Charlie Sang a Song,* by H. R. Hays and Daniel

Illustration by Uri Shulevitz for CHARLEY SANG A SONG by H. R. Hays and Daniel Hays.
Pictures copyright © 1964 by Uri Shulevitz. Reprinted with permission of Harper & Row,
Publishers.

Hays, often uses the reed pen to create his sketches. His figures reveal more action than do Low's or Bemelmans', however. All three artists have minimized the photographic function of painting and have traveled toward abstraction. None of the art by the three is entirely lacking in representative form, for too much of the objective forms is suggested in their style.

In a style suggestive of Vincent Van Gogh (especially his painting, *The Starry Night*), Blair Lent depicts stirring action in water, clouds, and smoke. His effective use of swirls to denote the forcefulness of the tidal wave can be noticed in *The Wave*, Margaret Hodges' adaptation of Lafcadio Hearn's *Gleanings in Buddha-fields*. The expressionistic illustrations in this version of the Japanese folktale were made by Lent with cardboard cuts and color overlays. He has also used this same technique effectively for *Baba Yaga*, a Russian folktale retold by Ernest Small. Baba Yaga, a fascinating and harmless witch who likes only bad children, literally swirls through the pages of this picture book.

Illustration by Blair Lent for BABA YAGA by Ernest Small. Pictures copyright © 1966 by Blair Lent. Reprinted with permission of Houghton Mifflin Company.

Often an expressionistic painting or sculpture is marked by elongations and distortions, linearity and pointedness, as in the figures that make up the battlescenes in *The Charge of the Light Brigade*. The men and the horses in the Provensens' paintings typify the nonphotographic quality of an expressionistic work. Intricate ornamentation is stripped away, and the artists appear to be far more concerned with the emotional message of Tennyson's lyrics than they are with the qualities that would imitate the reality of the soldiers' features, garb, and fighting equipment, or with the qualities that would imitate the real shape of the horses or their battle gear. This kind of modern expressionism is also used effectively by Alice and Martin Provensen in *The Golden Bible for Children; the New Testament* and in the attractive little book entitled *The First Noel; from the Gospel of St. Luke*. Their style of art reflects the acceptance of the directness typical of the primitive or elemental foundation, but it also strongly adheres to the idea that an essential expressive form is basic to the artistic creation. Their work in *The Charge of the Light Brigade* particularly, is marked by its directness and simplicity. The artists, using gouache, do pleasing colorwork.

If we compare the Provensens' paintings with Miroslav Sasek's work, we will see that, although their paintings definitely differ in many respects, their style must be grouped under the term "expressionistic art." Sasek's stylized elongations, and the distortions of the human figure, buildings, and animals lean toward the subjective and imaginative. The virile color pattern paintings and the almost bold simplification of his forms bring forth from his readers a strong, almost overwhelmingly forceful reaction to the "personality" of each city he describes in his series. The art in Sasek's books is evidence of his vitality and creative accomplishment. One quickly recognizes why his series of guidebooks for children delights even adults.

Taro Yashima (Jun Iwamatsu) is one of the most talented expressionistic painters and illustrators of children's books. The tremendously expressive illustrations in *Umbrella* and *Plenty to Watch* were done in brush and pencil, media which Taro Yashima handles to perfection. In each book, the illustrations denote distinctive action and evoke high-powered emotionalism on the part of the readers.

The watercolor paintings that appear in *The Dead Bird* by Margaret Wise Brown were done by Remy Charlip. His style is quite suggestive of the Mexican fresco artist, Diego Rivera (especially Rivera's fresco entitled *The Night of the Poor*). Charlip's style is indeed different from Sasek's or Alice and Martin Provensen's; and yet it is classified as expressionistic art. Emotionalism prevails in *The Dead Bird*. The illustrations so graphically portray the *feelings* of the children when they find the dead bird and indulge in the funeral service, and then soon forget about the incident as they resume their play. Charlip eliminates unnecessary detail and reduces shadows. His outlines, unlike those in Taro Yashima's paintings, are firm and clear. The delightful simplicity and naïveté of children are understandingly emphasized in the illustrations by expressionist, Remy Charlip.

Cubism. The cubist's paintings of the human figure and of landscapes are composed throughout of planes with curved or straight edges, but the figure or landscape is broken into its theoretical components. Each component is analyzed and split into prismatic shapes. The cubist's work is a construction of abstracted elements with colors used to unify the painting. The styles of Paul Cézanne and Wassily Kandinsky, in whose work the cubists found the basic principle of their formula, are both reflected in the paintings done by Brian Wildsmith. The works of these three artists evidence a quality that is structural and geometric. When their paintings are analyzed, one can only conclude that their works present poised forms and an organized structure. The fundamental idea behind this structure and order is that the artist feels that, in his paintings, he must rearrange the planes of an object in order to give his emotional or aesthetic response to it. Thus cubism is a form of expressionism. In many of the illustrations of Robert Louis Stevenson's

Illustration by Brian Wildsmith for A CHILD'S GARDEN OF VERSES by Robert Lewis Stevenson. Copyright © in this edition. Oxford University Press, 1966. Reprinted with permission of Franklin Watts, Inc.

A *Child's Garden of Verses,* and throughout all of *Brian Wildsmith's 1 2 3's,* Wildsmith employs a simplified sort of cubism. None of his figures disorganizes the planes of reality or rearranges them in an arbitrary order as was done by Picasso or by Albert Gleizes.

Most cubists renounce the aid of color and work in tones of brown and gray. Not Brian Wildsmith! He uses brilliant shades of green, lavender, blue, red, yellow, and pink. As Cézanne did, Wildsmith uses color to build structurally and to help with aesthetic organization of his painting. Perspective in Wildsmith's paintings is largely a matter of colors carefully chosen; it is not a matter of a vanishing point. The greatness of cubist painting usually lies in its structure, in the way in which shapes and masses fit together. Its greatness seldom lies in the use of color. Wildsmith has not mastered the technique of cubism to the extent that Kandinsky, Picasso, or Cézanne have mastered it. His paintings do not evoke the emotional response as do those of the artists just mentioned, probably because he depends too heavily upon color to present his message and is too conservative in his rearrangement of the planes of his objects. Nonetheless, he has introduced cubism to young children in a very adequate and agreeable form.

The influence of the cubists, Paul Kandinsky and Kasimir Malevich, is evidenced in the pictures made by Paul Rand, particularly in the illustrations that appear in *I Know a Lot of Things* by Ann and Paul Rand. Rand's pictures are in bright colors, and they convey the feeling of wonderment at the things a child can find in the world around him and the delight he experiences with his increasing knowledge.

Collage. Collage is a form of synthetic cubism, and Georges Braque and Picasso are the master-names of this style. A collage is made by pasting non-painterly materials onto swatches of pages and by completing the image with a linear structure drawn on top of these surfaces. Collage is a form of expressionism. Ezra Jack Keats and Leo Lionni are two of the many contemporary illustrators of children's books who use this technique. Keats, the recipient of the Caldecott Medal for *The Snowy Day,* has vigor, joyous color, and attractive organizational form in most of his illustrations. When making the pictures for *The Snowy Day,* he used wallpaper, angel hair, cotton, and other materials in addition to the painting. The collage done by Leo Lionni, author-illustrator of the delightful picture book entitled *Frederick,* is very appropriate for use in children's books. His designs are much simpler than those of Keats and are characterized by their simple but sophisticated understatement. The style of his pictures is not quite as vigorous and detailed as the style of Keats, but it does suit the stories it illustrates.

Illustration for FREDERICK, written and illustrated by Leo Lionni. Copyright © 1967 by Leo Lionni. Reprinted with permission of Pantheon Books, a Division of Random House, Inc.

Impressionistic Art. The impressionists emphasize the importance of color and light. They tend to tell their story through the use of "broken color." The impressionists often use dots and short dashes of pure pigment in close juxtaposition. Most often, their pictures emphasize the vibrant character of animate and inanimate things. They combine colors to produce living, palpitating shadows. In the impressionistic illustrations that are found in children's books, one quickly notices that a modern feeling of informality and detachment prevails. The impressionist does not seem to be concerned with the objects as such. He paints them as he perceives them at the moment, fleeting as that glimpse might be. The impressionistic painting must be viewed either from a distance or through squinted eyes. If one looks at it closely, he sees only the artist's dots or comma-like strokes. Typical of the impressionistic paintings are some of the works of Vincent Van Gogh, Claude Monet, Pablo Picasso, and Cézanne.

One need only examine the illustrations of "Looking-Glass River" or "The Cow" which appear in *A Child's Garden of Verses* by Robert Louis Stevenson to see the influence of the major impressionists on Brian Wildsmith. In these two illustrations, the lines are gone, and for the most part, form is lost in the atmosphere. Wildsmith uses fresh brilliant hues of almost every color of the spectrum to present a fresh look at a meadow filled with varied, beautiful flowers. His version is creative and visual. The spots and dashes of color that make up the floral mixture, juxtaposed on the canvas and merged by the eye, should delight his young readers.

Illustration by Brian Wildsmith for A CHILD'S GARDEN OF VERSES by Robert Lewis Stevenson. © Copyright in this edition. Oxford University Press. 1966. Reprinted with permission of Franklin Watts, Inc.

Pointillist Technique. In pointillism, which is a form of neo-impressionism, the picture is constructed with a color technique consisting of roughly equated dots. The eye blends one color with the other, thus giving form to the subject. The pictures are thoroughly planned and carefully controlled. The works of the master artist, Georges Seurat, (especially La Baignade) are examples of the pointillist technique. Pointillism depends upon the use of the original colors that make up the mixture. Examination of a picture done in this technique will usually reveal that it lacks the spontaneity and easygoing attitude that was common in the impressionists' paintings. Miroslav Sasek uses the pointillist technique occasionally in his series of guidebooks for children. In double-page spreads, he applies this technique to present many of the familiar landmarks and monuments found in the busy cities of Paris and London. The books are entitled *This is Paris* and *This is London,* respectively. In *This is New York,* he also uses pointillism in the pictures that portray the sun-seekers who swarm to the beach of Coney Island on a summer

Illustration by Margot Zemach for MAZEL AND SHLIMAZEL by Isaac Singer. Pictures copyright © 1967 by Margot Zemach. Reprinted with permission of Farrar, Straus & Giroux, Inc.

Sunday, and the thousands of baseball and football fans who crowd
Yankee Stadium to watch their heroes. Sasek's use of pointillism is somewhat modernized, however. The dots in his paintings are wider and
longer than those in the painting done by the originators of this technique.

Folk Art.   Usually, modern art is too cosmopolitan to be labeled
French art, English art, Russian art, and the like. Nonetheless, a nation
may have cultural standards and authorities strong enough to influence
the style of art used by its people. Each country has its folklore, and
traditionally, art is one form of folklore. Paintings which are not done
in the style of the cosmopolitan modernists reflect the moods, emotions,
and styles of thinking which are more common to a particular culture
group.

Margot Zemach's illustrations, which are done in ink line and wash,
present the authentic Eastern European art in *Mazel and Shlimazel; or
The Milk of a Lioness* by Isaac Bashevis Singer. Designed in large picture book format, this Yiddish fairy tale tells of the spirit of good fortune
and the spirit of bad luck and their rivalry over the fate of a simple
peasant boy.

In a stunning picture book entitled *The Nightingale,* by Hans Christian Andersen, and translated by Eva Le Gallienne, the illustrations by
Nancy Ekholm Burkert are done in a style reminiscent of early Chinese
screens. This is a book of rare beauty. It was an Honor Book in the
Spring Book Festival sponsored by the New York Herald Tribune in
1965 and was awarded the Gold Medal by the Society of Illustrators in
1966. The eight full-color, double-page spreads were done with brush
and colored India inks.

The illustrations for *Tico and the Golden Wings* are done in stylized
design and colors that are suggestive of the traditional art of India. Based
on a Hindu fable, this story of a bird who is different, and who gives
away his golden feathers in order to bring happiness to the needy, was
written and illustrated by the talented graphic artist, Leo Lionni.

Cartoon Style.   Cartoon art may be classified as a form of expressionistic art. The cartoon artist, like other expressionistic artists, gives
vent to his feelings and provokes an emotional response by means of his
sketches, but the emotionalism is usually expressed through or in some
form of humor. Two qualities are basic to cartoonism, and these qualities
provoke laughter, or at least a smile, from the reader. Incongruous and
incompatible characteristics or situations are depicted. Dr. Seuss (Theodore Seuss Geisel) has been successful as a cartoon artist and writer of
children's humorous stories. For example, the situations which Horton,

the faithful and persistent elephant, faces in *Horton Hatches the Egg* send youngsters into gales of laughter. Seuss sketched numerous wonderfully humorous and expressive pictures of this long-suffering creature. Horton, sitting on a small nest in a tree, at times looks bewildered, frightened, cold, or embarrassed. His facial expressions are indeed a delight to behold. The incongruity of such a situation as an elephant stranded on top of a tree in itself would amuse children. Scenes in which the tree (with Horton still sitting on the nest) is moved from the jungle and carried by boat across rolling and tossing ocean waters to America only to be sold to a circus, and the picture of the elephant-bird bursting out of the shell of the egg that Horton sat on so long and so faithfully, are other incongruities and incompatibilities in Seuss' cartoons that help to make this narrative enjoyable. Even primary age children recognize how ridiculous these situations are.

When depicting incongruities or incompatibilities, a cartoonist employs slapstick, the absurd, exaggerations and the like. The illustrations in *Bob Fulton's Amazing Soda-Pop Stretcher*, written by Jerome Beatty,

Illustration by Gahan Wilson for BOB FULTON'S AMAZING SODA-POP STRETCHER by Jerome Beatty, Jr. Copyright © 1963 by Jerome Beatty, Jr. Reprinted with permission of William R. Scott, Inc.

Jr., give evidence of these qualities. Gahan Wilson is the illustrator, and he has captured the absolute lunacy that permeates this wonderful parody on the politics and the scientific advances of the Space Age. It is a science-fiction story of Bob Fulton's accidental invention of a non-friction producing gook and how it gains the attention of our government as well as that of an enemy nation. The predicaments faced by Bob, the absurdities of the series of events that make up the story, and the simple sort of satire of this gay and exciting modern science-fiction novel are highlighted in Wilson's cartoon style illustrations. Especially clever are the illustrations of the two old maids, Ingrid and Annie, who knit secret messages into sweaters they send to Tierra Ninguno; of the amazingly wild bike ride taken by Bob's sister, Jennifer, when an explosion of the Pop Stretcher causes its gooey residue to spill onto the bearings and gears of her bike wheels; and of the number one spy of a foreign power who appears, dressed in black and with even his face daubed with black coloring.

Photographs. There is little or no doubt that a photograph can serve as an illustration. But, there is considerable debate as to whether or not a phtograph should be considered a work of art. Some people consider a photograph an impersonal mechanical record, a reproduction of the visual facts of an object, scene, or document. It may be used to make a written statement more concrete, or it may be used to clarify or extend that statement. The photograph is not the personal, subjective expression of a creative mind; it is not an expression of a subjective experience or feeling. Nonetheless, photographs can be used with marked artistic sensibility to illustrate literary content, theme, or mood.

Good photograph illustration is characterized by an acceptable rendering of highlight areas and shadow detail; that is, lighting and subject matter are rather contrasting. Silhouette images usually are to be avoided, especially when it is important that the reader notice details in the subject. The choice of background in a photograph is dependent upon the subject matter and upon the effect for which the illustrator is aiming. Nonetheless, the background should be even-toned and in contrast to the object that is photographed. In general, a dark object should have a light background, and a light object should have a dark background.

When one uses photographs to illustrate a story, he usually isolates or emphasizes important picture elements. He uses lighting, for example, to make certain parts of the picture stand out. Dare Wright tends to accomplish emphasis by photographing the objects (dolls) before a background of uniform tone. Ylla often used this same technique with her illustrations of animals. When background detail is present, it must serve to establish the setting and the atmosphere. It should be subdued or, perhaps, eliminated altogether. Sometimes the technique of selective focusing is used; that is, important aspects of the subject matter are in sharp focus, and the background is out of focus. Dare Wright and Ylla have used this technique, too, to accomplish emphasis.

Both of these illustrators limit the number of objects that they include within any one scene. As a result, their photographs are uncluttered and precise. The action that they illustrate is easily identifiable. This is an important characteristic of a photograph illustration.

Proportionately, there are far fewer children's books illustrated with photographs than those illustrated with other kinds of pictures. Most of the books that are illustrated with photographs are informational books rather than bona fide literary selections. There are quite a few poetry anthologies, however, especially anthologies of *haiku* and modern verse, that are illustrated with photographs.

The photographs that illustrate Thomas Matthiesen's books, *A B C, An Alphabet Book* and *Things to See; A Child's World of Familiar Objects* are in color. These pictures are photographs of objects that can be identified by most children. They are reproduced in bright colors and are appealing and attractive.

Numerous striking photographs (many of them scenes rather than single objects) complement or extend the poems that are included in *Reflections on a Gift of Watermelon Pickle . . . and Other Modern Verse,* an anthology of modern verse, compiled by Stephen Dunning et al. The poems in another anthology entitled *The Wind and the Rain* and compiled by Richard Lewis, reveal child-like responses to nature, and the accompanying photographs by Helen Buttfield complement these poems which were written by children from age five to thirteen.

The black and white photographs of the art objects that are described in Shirley Glubok's books are well-reproduced. In each case, the artifacts (ornaments, temples, jewelry, statues, etc.) are strikingly displayed. Included in her art series are *The Art of Ancient Mexico* and *The Art of the Etruscans.* The photography for each of these books was done by Alfred H. Tamarin.

National Aeronautics and Space Administration photographs were used to illustrate Gene Gurney's *Walk in Space; the Story of Project Gemini.* These photographs clarify the author's reviews of the aims and accomplishments of Project Gemini, of the specific purposes and achievements of each flight, and of the actions of the astronauts and the ground tracking crews.

Summary. It is in the arrangement of line and color that the style of art can be identified. The various styles of art used by graphic artists to suggest and evoke the content and other narrative elements of literature include the following: representational art, expressionistic art, cubism, collage, impressionistic art, pointillism, folk art, cartoon style art, and photography. Style in illustrative are is a rather elusive quality, but the author has attempted to describe some of the characteristics of each style and to cite exemplary publications in which each of these styles was used. The style of art which is used to illustrate a book may be influenced by several factors such as the content and the mood of the story, the age of the reader, the artist's concept of his anticipated audience, the basic personality of the artist, his creative talent, and the media used to make the pictures, as well as the artist's mastery of the media technique employed.

SELECTED REFERENCES

ANDERSEN, HANS CHRISTIAN. *The Nightingale.* Translated by Eva Le Gallienne. Illustrated by Nancy Ekholm Burkert. New York: Harper & Row, Publishers, Inc., 1965.
———. *Thumbelina.* Illustrated by Adrienne Adams. New York: Charles Scribner's Sons, 1961.
ASBJÖRNSEN, P. C. and MOE, J. E. *The Three Billy Goats Gruff.* Illustrated by Marcia Brown. New York: Harcourt, Brace & World, Inc., 1957.
BEATTY, JEROME, JR. *Bob Fulton's Amazing Soda-Pop Stretcher.* Illustrated by Gahan Wilson. New York: William R. Scott, Inc., Publisher, 1963.
BEMELMANS, LUDWIG. *Madeline.* New York: The Viking Press, Inc., 1939.
BROWN, MARCIA. *Cinderella.* New York: Charles Scribner's Sons, 1954.
———. *Once a Mouse—A Fable Cut in Wood.* New York: Charles Scribner's Sons, 1961.
BROWN, MARGARET WISE. *The Dead Bird.* Illustrated by Remy Charlip. New York: William R. Scott, Inc., 1958.
DE LA MARE, WALTER. *Jack and the Beanstalk.* Illustrated by Joseph Low. New York: Alfred A. Knopf, Inc., 1959.
DUNNING, STEPHEN, et al. *Reflections on a Gift of Watermelon Pickle . . . . and Other Modern Verse.* Illustrated with photographs. Glenview, Ill.: Scott, Foresman & Company, 1966.
FRASCONI, ANTONIO. *See Again, Say Again.* New York: Harcourt, Brace & World, 1964.
GLUBOK, SHIRLEY. *The Art of Ancient Mexico.* Photographs by Alfred H. Tamarin. New York: Harper & Row, Publishers, 1968.
———. *The Art of Etruscans.* Photographs by Alfred H. Tamarin. New York: Harper & Row, Publishers, 1967.
GOUDEY, ALICE. *Butterfly Time.* Illustrated by Adrienne Adams. New York: Charles Scribner's Sons, 1964.
———. *Houses from the Sea.* Illustrated by Adrienne Adams. New York: Charles Scribner's Sons, 1959.
GURNEY, GENE. *Walk in Space; the Story of Project Gemini.* Illustrated with photographs. (Landmark Books) New York: Random House, Inc., 1967.
HAYS, H. R., and DANIEL. *Charlie Sang a Song.* Illustrated by Uri Shulevitz. New York: Harper & Row, Publishers, 1964.
HODGES, MARGARET. *The Wave.* Illustrated by Blair Lent. Boston: Houghton Mifflin Company, 1964.
KEATS, EZRA JACK. *The Snowy Day.* New York: The Viking Press, Inc., 1962.
LEWIS, RICHARD. *The Wind and the Rain.* Photographs by Helen Buttfield. New York: Simon & Schuster, Inc., 1968.

LIONNI, LEO. *Frederick*. New York: Pantheon Books, A Division of Random House, Inc., 1967.

————. *Tico and the Golden Wings*. New York: Pantheon Books, A Division of Random House, Inc., 1964.

MATTHIESEN, THOMAS. *A B C; An Alphabet Book*. New York: Platt & Munk, Inc., 1966.

————. *Things to See; A Child's World of Familiar Objects*. New York: Platt & Munk, Inc., 1966.

McNEER, MAY. *The American Indian Story*. Illustrated by Lynd Ward. New York: Farrar, Straus & Giroux, Inc., 1963.

————. *The Canadian Story*. Illustrated by Lynd Ward. New York: Farrar Straus & Giroux, Inc., 1950.

PROVENSEN, ALICE and MARTIN. *The First Noel; from the Gospel of St. Luke*. New York: Golden Press, Inc., 1954.

RAND, ANN and PAUL. *I Know a Lot of Things*. Illustrated by Paul Rand. New York: Harcourt, Brace & World, Inc., 1956.

SASEK, MIROSLAV. *This is London*. New York: The Macmillan Company, 1959.

————. *This is New York*. New York: The Macmillan Company, 1960.

————. *This is Paris*. New York: The Macmillan Company, 1959.

SCHLEIN, MIRIAM. *The Big Cheese*. Illustrated by Joseph Low. New York: William R. Scott, Inc., 1958.

SEUSS, DR. *Horton Hatches the Egg*. New York: Random House, Inc., 1940.

SINGER, ISAAC BASHEVIS. *Mazel and Shlimazel; or The Milk of a Lioness*. Illustrated by Margot Zemach. New York: Farrar, Straus, & Giroux, Inc., 1967.

SMALL, ERNEST. *Baba Yaga*. Illustrated by Blair Lent. Boston: Houghton Mifflin Company, 1966.

STEVENSON, ROBERT LOUIS. *A Child's Garden of Verses*. Illustrated by Brian Wildsmith. New York: Franklin Watts, Inc., 1966.

TENNYSON, ALFRED LORD. *The Charge of the Light Brigade*. Illustrated by Alice and Martin Provensen. New York: Golden Press, Inc., 1964.

TUDOR, TASHA. *A Is for Annabelle*. New York: Henry Z. Walck, Inc., 1954.

————. *Around the Year*. New York: Henry Z. Walck, Inc., 1957.

————. *1 Is One*. New York: Henry Z. Walck, Inc., 1956.

————. *Becky's Birthday*. New York: The Viking Press, 1960.

WARD, LYND. *The Biggest Bear*. Boston: Houghton Mifflin Company, 1952.

WERNER, ELSA JANE, ed. *The Golden Bible for Children; the New Testament*. Illustrated by Alice and Martin Provensen. New York: Golden Press, Inc., 1953.

WILDSMITH, BRIAN. *Brian Wildsmith's 1, 2, 3's*. New York: Franklin Watts, Inc., 1965.

YASHIMA, MITSU and TARO. *Plenty to Watch*. New York: The Viking Press, Inc., 1954.

YASHIMA, TARO. *Umbrella*. New York: The Viking Press, Inc., 1958.

chapter 3

the artists' media and techniques

A picture is a language. The book artist expresses his thoughts and feelings in this language through effective use of the various painterly and graphic techniques. His facility and skill at expressing himself in this language is evaluated largely in terms of the way he uses his media to reveal his understanding of the function of form, his sensitivity to the flow of line, his originality, and his mastery of the media itself. These powers are revealed in the pictures he creates for an illustrated book. There is a wide variety of media available to the book artist. The subject of the book itself is often a major determinant of the art medium that is best to use to create the illustrations for that book.

The author of an art education book for children told her young readers that the medium an artist uses changes the appearance of a picture as well as influences the way one feels about a picture.[1] The artist may use pastels, watercolors, oil paints, pencil, crayon, tempera, gouache, or ink. He may use techniques such as woodcuts, wood engravings, linoleum cuts, paper etchings, scratchboard, or stone lithograph to make his picture. The medium determines, in large measure, the lines and shapes the artist will use to make his design. It limits the extent to which he will use hatching, crosshatching, scribbles, smudges, or washes in his drawings. It follows, then, that the materials and techniques used by the artist to create his visual images may affect the manner and extent to which the literary functions of his pictures are accomplished.

That the same story may inspire different artists in different ways is a fairly well accepted fact. Scores of studies made by students of psychology and of human growth and development substantiate the

---

[1]Helen Borten. *A Picture Has a Special Look*. (New York: Abelard-Schuman Limited, 1961), unpaged.

principle of individual differences and uniqueness of personality. These studies point out the inherent differences among or between members of a group as well as differences within a given individual in capacity and performance. Research has also revealed that human variations are caused by the range of experiences and the expectations or environmental demands that are made upon individuals.

It is not at all surprising, then, that artists reading the same story will evidence through their drawings differences in perception. One artist will decide that woodcuts would be the best medium to present the message of the story, a second artist will decide that watercolors would best serve this purpose, and a third artist will think a collage technique would be best. Each artist has read the same story, and yet each will identify different aspects of importance in the story. Each will come away with different recollections and different concepts. Each will probably decide upon a different art medium to be used to make the illustrations. But even if they all agreed on the same medium, in all probability, each artist would employ a markedly different style of art, and each would use a different combination of colors. The illustrations prepared by each artist would highlight the same details of the story in an entirely different manner.

Regardless of the media used to make the pictures, the book illustrator must be able to express the individuality of his style. A woodcut print by Evaline Ness will be different from a woodcut print by Gil Miret, Ed Emberley, Antonio Frasconi, or Nonny Hogrogian. Likewise, the watercolor paintings done by Leo Politi will differ in elements of style from the pictures done in the same medium by Alois Carigiet, Ludwig Bemelmans, or Adrienne Adams. Scratchboard illustrations done by Barbara Cooney will differ from those done by Leonard Everett Fisher.

Consider the varied graphic interpretations brought to the Mother Goose rhymes. Tasha Tudor is a watercolor artist who has used her medium to create delicate and quaint interpretations of the well-known rhymes. Far more sophisticated in his treatment of these same rhymes is Brian Wildsmith, who used gouache to create his paintings. *In a Pumpkin Shell* is another Mother Goose book. It was illustrated by Joan Walsh Anglund who used pen-and-ink drawings and watercolors to make her detailed and ingenuous pictures. Philip Reed made colored wood engravings for the illustrations in *Mother Goose and Nursery Rhymes.*

Blair Lent used cardboard cutouts and overlay wash to make the illustrations that appear in *The Wave,* Margaret Hodges' version of the Japanese folktale that tells about an old man who set fire to his rice fields on the mountain to save the villagers from a tidal wave. Pastels were used by Mamoru Funai for Sara Cone Bryant's version of this same folktale. Funai's illustrations are handsome and original as are Lent's, and yet Funai's work is far less expressionistic than is Lent's. The work of the former is more appropriate for younger children than is that of the latter. The style of the one artist has an immediate direct appeal; that of the other is more subtle and sophisticated. The one makes use of the primary colors; the other uses subdued colors.

Some artists can work with a multiplicity of media and are not tied to any one process. The mood of the story itself will determine the medium the artist employs. The artist himself must believe that for him no other medium would be as effective as the one he chooses to tell a particular story. He must be able to exploit the qualities that make this particular medium unique. He must be able to make this medium say better what another medium could say only adequately.

Marcia Brown uses a variety of media to create her illustrations, and she uses each medium to the greatest possible advantage. She uses linoleum block cuts, woodcuts, flat color, gouache and crayon over rubber cement, casein, ink, and watercolors. These are not all the media she uses to make the pictures for her books, but it is obvious that a single artist, like Marcia Brown, can be versatile in the media she uses and yet master the technique for each. Marcia Brown has varied the media for her many books, but in each case, she has chosen a medium that has permitted her to meet the requirements she thought were demanded by each story. She has said that the artist should use the media (means) that will permit him to say what he has to say and

> The means will always be determined by the subject at hand, and that is why I feel that each book should look different from the others, whether or not the medium used is the same. . . .A technique learned as a formula to apply willy-nilly to any subject often knocks the life out of the subject. The vitality, the quality peculiar to the subject should dictate the method to follow . . .[2]

Barbara Cooney also tries to fit the medium and technique to the demands of the story. She has used pen and ink, pen and ink with wash, casein, collage, watercolors, acrylics, scratchboard, and lithographs. Evaline Ness, too, has used a wide variety of media but is better known for her work done in line and wash, collage, and woodcuts.

There is no doubt that, before the book artist selects the art medium to make his drawings, he must be able to visualize the images suggested

---

[2]Marcia Brown. "Integrity and Intuition," in Bertha M. Miller and Eleanor Field. *Caldecott Medal Books: 1938-1957.* (Boston: The Horn Book, 1957), pp. 267-277.

in a manuscript. It is equally important that he have a mastery of paint-erly or graphic technique(s) so that he can make a meaningful and creative graphic statement of the story.

The book artist of today is given considerable freedom in his selec-tion of media, but Goethe once said, "It is only within limits that the master is evidenced." The book artist of today has to realize his own strengths and weaknesses as they pertain to the use of a particular art medium. Also, he has to be fully aware of the limitations, the possibili-ties, the advantages of the medium that he uses to deliver an author's message and his own message.

Because an artist does have the freedom to use the medium that he can handle well and that he feels will best help him interpret the text, and because most artists today are technically skilled in using varied art media, the quality of book illustration in this country is at a respect-able level. In fact, the work done by many of the book artists of today is characterized by integrity and a certain self-assurance. It reflects sin-cere and uninhibited efforts by the artists. The practice of using a variety of media to illustrate children's books has encouraged much diversity in the styles of art employed by the illustrators of children's books. Diver-sity in the media, techniques, and art styles that book artists may use to make pictures for children's books tends to increase the competition in this aspect of publication of children's books. Certainly it brings forth a wider range of talents and ideas to the field of children's literature than ever before. This should help to bring more and better books to young readers.

Painterly Techniques

Paint is powder color mixed with a binding medium. One can paint with an oil medium, with watercolor, or with pastel. Each painter has his personal color sense. Each one tends to use and mix a range of colors in his own way, some artists being more timid (or aggressive) than others in the color range. Most artists do go far beyond the four process colors (red, blue, yellow, and black). Seldom are they reluctant to mix these pigments, and so they do come up with various gradations of the secondary colors.

Watercolor. Watercolor, which is powder color bound with gum arabic and glycerine, is applied in washes. It is a transparent medium, and one which is not the most popular with contemporary book artists, probably because it is not as vigorous as the other media. Artists who have used watercolor to make the original paintings for the pictures that illustrate children's books include Leo Politi, Adrienne Adams, Tasha

Tudor, and Maurice Sendak. A few of the books illustrated by each of
these book artists are discussed in the pages that follow.

Leo Politi was awarded the Caldecott Medal in 1950 for his illustrations in *Song of the Swallows.* Occasionally, he has mixed white with
watercolors but, in the main, his medium is watercolor. One would
probably conclude after having examined the illustrations in *Juanita,
Little Leo, Pedro, the Angel of Olvera Street,* and *Saint Francis and the
Animals* that his illustrations are composed with a quiet deliberation. It
seems that his style is quite stabilized as is the medium he uses in his
work. His illustrations are deceptively simple. In fact, there is a primitive
look about many of his pictures. Particularly noticeable are the stylized
lumbering figures, the oversized, stiff hands and feet, qualities so characteristic of the primitives. Politi does not include much detail in his work.
Indeed, his illustrations are characterized by an economy of detail. Nonetheless, there is considerable action depicted in his paintings, and there
is enough suggestion for the child's imagination to expand. He includes
enough of detail and attention to human features to give an adequate
picture of people in their environment. Politi uses an assortment of tone
and color in his pictures. Even when limited to two colors, he manages to
produce considerable diversity in shades. His use of color to denote mood
and time of day is skillful. He uses black and white or dark colors for
evening scenes; for gay moods, he uses the brighter shades; and for sad-
ness, he uses the darker shades.

Politi's illustrations can be contrasted with those made by Adrienne
Adams who also uses watercolor in many of her pictures. Both artists
often work in full color. Miss Adams' work was also recognized by the
book critics as being outstanding, for her illustrations in *Houses from the
Sea* and *The Day We Saw the Sun Come Up,* both written by Alice E.
Goudey, were runners-up for the Caldecott Medal awarded in 1960 and
in 1962, respectively. Miss Adams' paintings are representational and
winsome. She uses delicate, clear colors, and her work is detailed and
exact. The illustrations of seashells in *Houses from the Sea* are so authentic in each detail that they could be referred to as a quick guide for
identification of the more common shells—moon shells, jingle shells,
cockleshells, cowrie shells, periwinkle shells, and so on. This meticulous
attention to detail is also given to her illustrations for folktales. For example, the figures in *The Shoemaker and the Elves* are clothed in authentic costumes for the period in which the Grimm brothers were col-
lecting the folktales. The drawings in *The Shoemaker and the Elves* were
executed in crayon and watercolor. The delicate and bright details found
in Hans Christian Andersen's *Thumbelina* highlight the imaginary quality
of this enchanting fairytale. The key drawings for this story were done in

Illustration by Adrienne Adams for THUMBELINA by Hans Christian Andersen, translated by R. P. Keigwin. Illustrations copyright © 1961 by Adrienne Adams. Reprinted with permission of Charles Scribner's Sons.

pencil and watercolor wash. The pencil, which can also be a delicate instrument for art work, helps Adrienne Adams to carry out the relaxed detail that is characteristic of her watercolor paintings.

Alois Carigiet uses vivid and brilliant watercolors in his book illustrations. A recipient of the Hans Christian Andersen Award[3] in 1966, Carigiet is far more expressionistic in his style than Politi. His illustrations for A Bell for Ursli and The Snowstorm highlight the gaiety of the Swiss festival for which the children in the stories are preparing. Many of his

[3]The Hans Christian Andersen Award is an international award, given every two years, by the International Board on Books for Young People. Carigiet was recognized as an artist who contributed significantly to children's literature through his illustrations.

illustrations in *A Bell for Ursli* and *The Snowstorm,* as well as in *Florina and the Wild Bird,* all written by Selina Chonz, are sumptuous full-color spreads. Each is suggestive of a huge mural. Carigiet's scenes of the Swiss villages and mountains portray Switzerland as a "paradise" that one must be certain to visit as soon as possible.

Another recognized watercolor artist is Tasha Tudor. Like Adrienne Adams, she uses pencil along with watercolors and is equally exacting and detailed in her approach. Examination of the features of her book characters, the clothing they wear, the interior settings, the landscape scenes, and her sketches of flowers and animals reveal that Tasha Tudor is a meticulous draftsman. She employs the representational style of art in her painting, and the general tenor of her work is quaint and quiet. Her approach to illustration is highly decorative. Her drawings express a make-believe quality because they include realistic and romantic excesses. This quality is seen in her illustrations for Andersen's fairy tales as well as for books classified as here-and-now stories, *Pumpkin Moonshine, Linsey Woolsey,* or the concept books, *Around the Year, 1 is One,* and *A is for Annabelle.* The feeling that pervades throughout Tasha Tudor's books is that of serenity and quietness, a mood quite contrary to that depicted by numerous contemporary artists who reveal their tenseness and need for activity through the use of bold colors, loose forms, and heavy lines in their paintings. Tasha Tudor's illustrations would probably be more appealing to little girls than to boys, for they are so very feminine, so soft and delicate. In the delightfully attractive picture book entitled *A is for Annabelle,* she uses an old-fashioned doll with all her belongings to present the alphabet. The figures of the children who appear in the illustrations of *1 is One,* where numbers one through twenty are presented in verse form, are clothed in old-fashioned garments typical of the nineteenth century, a not too uncommon habit with Tasha Tudor.

There are other artists who have used watercolors skillfully in their book illustrations. This art medium was used by Hardie Gramatky to create the gay cartoon-like illustrations that appear in *Little Toot* and *Bolivar.* Elmer and Berta Hader used watercolors and pencil to make the realistic drawings for *The Big Snow,* for which they were awarded the Caldecott Medal in 1949. Another Caldecott Medal book which is illustrated with watercolor paintings is *Time of Wonder* by Robert McCloskey. The illustrations in this book are done in an expressionistic style.

Pencil and watercolors were used by Marvin Bileck to create the fanciful and unbelievably detailed illustrations for the nonsense book by Julian Scheer entitled *Rain Makes Applesauce* which was a runner-up for the Caldecott Medal in 1966 and was cited by the *New York Times* in 1965 as one of the "Ten Best Illustrated Children's Books." The late Francoise (pseud. Francoise Seignobosc), author-illustrator of the Jeanne-Marie series for the nursery school audience, used watercolors to create her peasant-like drawings. The colors are cheery, and bright, and yet not brilliant. The figures are doll-like and simple. *Jeanne-Marie Counts Her Sheep, The Thank-You Book, The Things I Like* and *Noel for Jeanne-Marie* seem to be among her most popular books.

Gouache and Poster Color. Gouache is powder color mixed with an opaque white, usually Chinese white; poster color is a coarser version of gouache. Actually, watercolor, gouache, and poster color are the same medium, the only difference being that in the latter two media, there is an addition of the white filling. Often, a gouache painting looks like an oil painting. In the examples cited in the pages that follow, a few artists who use gouache and poster paint are identified.

Roger Duvoisin used gouache in the drawings for Alvin Tresselt's *Hide and Seek Fog,* an exquisite mood picture book. So expressionistic are these full-color paintings that one can almost feel the fog roll in from the sea, or hang wet and dripping from the articles of clothing hung on the clothesline. The use of hazy pearl gray throughout the book contributes to the effectiveness of this expressionistic art piece.

It is hard to believe that this same medium was used by Brian Wildsmith in his number and alphabet books or in the truly stunning book entitled *Brian Wildsmith's Birds.* Quite in keeping with the form of expressionistic art which he uses, namely a modern and simple sort of cubism, is the use of the wide array of brilliant and subdued colors present in all of his books. Tasha Tudor's quaint, quiet, and controlled type of illustrations were described above as being indicative of a make-believe or ideal world of the nineteenth century. One might say that Brian Wildsmith's use of form and color symbolizes the busy, uninhibited, and educated twentieth century.

Full-color gouache was used in Alice and Martin Provensen's illustrations that appear in *The Charge of the Light Brigade,* a stunning expressionistic version of the well-known poem by Alfred Lord Tennyson. The double spread colored paintings serve to justify the hostile and disgruntled feelings that permeated the ranks of the servicemen during the Crimean War after the disastrous British cavalry charge against the Russian batteries at Balaclava in 1854. The effective splashes of blue, red, and brown depict booming cannons, wounded and fallen soldiers, falling or wildly hysterical horses, as well as the arrogant, determined military leaders—all so very typical of this grim historical event. This

Illustration by Alice and Martin Provensen, from CHARGE OF THE LIGHT BRIGADE by
Alfred Lord Tennyson. Reproduced with permission © copyright 1964 by Golden Press, Inc.

book, by the way, exemplifies unusual book design. The text of the poem
is done in Victorian script and looks like hand-lettering, thus emphasiz-
ing the fact that the servicemen carried handwritten copies of Tennyson's
poem with them. The cover is a collage consisting of newspaper articles
which had reported the tragic battle. The size of the book, the quality
of paper used, and the physical arrangement of each page evidence careful and skillful bookmaking. The Provensens also used gouache to make
the drawings for *The Golden Bible for Children; the New Testament*
which was included in the American Institute of Graphic Arts Children's
Book Show in 1954.

Gouache was used by Aliki, (pseud. Aliki Brandenberg) in the
drawings for *A Weed is a Flower, the Life of George Washington Carver*.
An understated simplicity characterizes Aliki's use of color and line.
This approach is compatible with the brief, charmingly simple and
dignified biography of the Negro research scientist, George Washington
Carver.

Storm'd at with shot and shell,
While horse and hero fell,
They that had fought so well
Came thro' the jaws of Death,
Back from the mouth of hell,
All that was left of them,
Left of six hundred.

Another book artist who uses gouache is the talented Leonard Weisgard who used this medium for the illustrations that appear in the 1947 Caldecott Medal book, *The Little Island,* by Golden MacDonald. He painted his pictures on pressed wood that had been covered with a layer of lead white and lightly sanded. On every other page are five colorful illustrations; the alternate pages are two-color duotones. Each one is a beautiful picture.

Duvoisin and Weisgard use the same medium, and yet each has come up with strikingly different effects. Weisgard's drawings in *The Little Island* are representational in style and, in general, the colors are brilliant and sparkling. The art style used by Duvoisin in *Hide and Seek Fog* is expressionistic, and colors are muted and hazy. In *The Little Island,* Weisgard has included more decorative details than he has in more recent books. Duvoisin's book lacks the decorative quality. One would readily recognize the unique creative talents of Weisgard and Duvoisin if they compared only the mist scenes contained in *The Little*

Island and in *Hide and Seek Fog*. Each artist used gouache, but the feelings each artist expresses about fog and mist are quite different; and yet each interpretation is compatible with the particular story the artist has illustrated. Weisgard also used gouache to make the pictures for Margaret Wise Brown's *The Golden Bunny* which was included in the American Institute of Graphic Arts Children's Book Show in 1954.

Celestino Piatti used poster color to make the beautiful illustrations in *The Happy Owls, Celestino Piatti's Animal ABC,* and *The Holy Night*. The text of the latter was written by Aurel von Jüchen and translated from the German by Cornelia Schaeffer. Piatti uses a considerable

amount of color in all of his paintings, and his drawings are all solid and bold. Those in *The Holy Night* are "atmospheric." When taken individually, the pictures are strikingly handsome; but collectively, these richly-colored paintings tend to overpower the simple and brief story, or informative text, in each of the books they illustrate.

Jacob Lawrence is one of America's foremost Negro painters. He used poster color to make the expressionistic pictures that illustrate the moving narrative verse in *Harriet and the Promised Land*. The stylized drawings, the exaggerated features of the characters, the brilliant and flat shades of color all contribute to make this artist's work beautifully artistic and noteworthy.

Tempera. Tempera is a painterly technique used by numerous contemporary book artists. It is powder color ground in water and mixed with an albuminous, gelatinous or colloidal medium. Tempera is not particularly difficult to work with. Its opacity can be increased or lessened at the will of a skillful artist, as can the brightness and shades of various colors be controlled. This medium permits carefully detailed work if the artist wishes to paint in this manner, but it also allows for loose, uninhibited brush strokes should the artist prefer that approach. Some of the major book artists who have used tempera for their medium include Nicolas Sidjakov, Maurice Sendak, and Bruno Munari.

Handsome drawings are found in *Baboushka and the Three Kings* which was illustrated by Nicolas Sidjakov, who used tempera and felt

Illustration by Nicolas Sidjakov for BABOUSHKA AND THE THREE KINGS by Ruth Robbins. Illustrations copyright © 1960 by Nicolas Sidjakov. Reprinted with permission of Parnassus Press.

pen in four bright colors to create his stylized wooden-like figures. Through his use of color and style, he has given a "Russian feeling" to this Russian folktale. Sidjakov uses tempera with a masculine sureness. Ruth Robbins is the author of this 1960 Caldecott Medal award winning book.

Maurice Sendak used tempera to paint the illustrations in *Where the Wild Things Are.* The drawings for this picture book were done in cartoon style. The creatures that Max meets in his fantasy world are grotesque, but they will probably delight almost any young reader and stimulate his imagination; very likely, they will humor him rather than frighten him. The playful mood and the fantasy in this picture book are fortified throughout by Sendak's brief but well-written text, his choice of colors, his style of drawing, and his use of white space.

Tempera was used for all the children's books that Bruno Munari illustrated. Worthy of note are the picture books entitled *Bruno Munari's ABC, Bruno Munari's Zoo, Who's There? Open the Door!* and *The Birthday Present.* His illustrations are very simple and are sharply drawn. Munari usually uses brilliant hues. Each book evidences a charming sense of humor that is certain to provoke smiles from the young reader. Each picture book reflects Munari's originality and skill as a book designer and his unique style as a tempera artist.

Pastel Painting.   Pastel consists of powder color mixed to the correct hue with white chalk and bound with gum tragacanth and liquids. (It is not merely white chalk stained with dye.) It is used dry, like a chalk. The artist can build up tone in delicate layers, usually on rough cardboard. Most often, the pastel is rubbed with the finger or a soft cloth. Whereas watercolor is transparent, pastel is opaque. It is also "soft"

Illustration by Mamoru Funai for THE BURNING RICE FIELDS by Sara Cone Bryant. Copyright © 1963 by Holt, Rinehart and Winston, Inc. Reprinted with permission of the publisher.

in appearance. Some artists claim that it is easier to use than watercolors, and that they like to use pastel because its effect is immediate and its use is more rapid than most other painterly techniques.

Pastels were used by Mamoru Funai to illustrate Sara Cone Bryant's *The Burning Rice Fields*, a version of a well-known Japanese legend. The texture of this art medium is apparent in Funai's sketches; the grain of the chalk can be seen, and it looks "soft and furry." Funai used pastels to create pictures that are characterized by a pleasant simplicity and forthrightness, qualities quite consistent with the author's brief and simple version of this folktale.

Nonny Hogrogian used pastels with pen and line drawings for the 1966 Caldecott Medal award book, *Always Room for One More* by Sorche Nic Leodhas. The touches of heather color and green pastels for the fields of heather serve to convey the atmosphere and beauty of Scotland. The use of pastels to create a background of heather-covered hills adds to the elegance of Miss Hogrogian's drawings which were done in pen-and-ink line and crosshatching.

Graphic Techniques

There is a wide range of printmaking materials that are used by contemporary artists to make surface relief paintings. Traditionally, woodcuts were the main medium used. Cardboard, composition board, plastic, plywood, and paper reliefs are the media used by many contemporary relief artists. These graphic techniques are discussed in the pages that follow. Stone lithography is a planographic, or surface, process of printmaking; print and non-print surfaces are on the same level. This technique for drawing will also be discussed in this chapter.

Woodcuts. The wood that is used for woodcuts must be cut from the length of the trunk of a tree. A design is usually cut crosswise to the natural grain of the wood and can be seen after the areas to be printed white are removed by the woodcutter's gouge and knife. Various types of wood may be used, but the plank must be well-seasoned and dry and must be neither too hard nor too soft. The most popular type of wood is pear wood, but pine wood is commonly used, too. Other woods that an artist may use are cherry, lime, and beach. Nonny Hogrogian used pear wood for the block from which the prints were pulled for the keepsakes that were given to the guests attending a Caldecott Medal award dinner. Ed Emberley prefers the pine plank.

The woodcut artist traces his drawing on the planed wood block in reverse. Thus, it will appear the right way in the print. Non-printing areas (those which will be printed white) are cut away with scoops and sharp knives; the printing areas (those which will be printed black) are the raised portions left standing. The effect of cutting a picture in wood is different from the effect of drawing a picture on canvas with a brush, a pen, or a pencil. In very general terms, the characteristic style of lines resulting from woodcutting is rather severe, powerful, and terse. Seldom can one cut lines that are delicate, supple, or fluid. These are characteristics of lines made in wood and apply when they are compared with lines made with more manipulative media such as pen or brush. Few people would say that the woodcuts made by Evaline Ness, Antonio Frasconi, or Ed Emberley are lacking in delicacy, suppleness, and mobility, for their work with wood is graceful and fluid. And so the characteristics of woodcut prints are made strictly in relative terms.

When the woodcut prints are to make use of more than one color, the artist is usually asked to make a separate woodcut drawing for each color. The final woodcut prints are submitted to the publisher as overlays. The works of a few of the major woodcut artists are discussed briefly below.

Evaline Ness used woodcut prints for the illustrations that appear in *Tom Tit Tot, Double Discovery*, and *Josephina February*. By and large, her woodcuts are fairly sophisticated in design. She evidences remarkable skill with the tools and is able to produce graceful and delicate lines with this art medium. The woodcuts that were made to illustrate *Josephina February* are especially effective. The pictures of the charming, skinny little Josephina with very unruly hair accentuate this compassionate story of a little Haitian girl who is faced with making a choice between the baby burro which she finds and grows to love, and a pair of real leather shoes for her grandfather. The style of Miss Ness' woodcuts and her use of color reflect the spirit of Haiti, its richness and its poverty, its beauty and its wretchedness. The woodcut prints that illustrate *Tom Tit Tot* effect a boisterously humorous mood. They are done in a far more uninhibited manner than those that were made to tell Josephina February's story. The pictures emphasize the qualities of each of the story characters—the greediness and gullibility of one, the dullness, awkwardness, and laziness of the other. Miss Ness' illustrations are quite compatible with the style of writing that Joseph Jacobs used in "Tom Tit Tot," his version of Rumpelstiltskin, a well-known folktale which he included in the anthology entitled *English Folk and Fairy Tales*.

Nonny Hogrogian uses free patterns in her woodcuts as she does in her line drawings. When she has an illustrating commission that calls for more than one color, making it necessary for her to use several wood blocks to build up a design, she positions one color in relation to the other by eye. She does not use guides. This is in contrast with the work done by woodcut artists Ed Emberley, Marcia Brown, or Evaline Ness whose designs are more exacting and call for a more careful use of guides in their overlays. Nonny Hogrogian studied under Antonio Frasconi at the New School for Social Research where she learned to do woodcuts.

Some of the books that Nonny Hogrogian illustrated with woodcuts include *The Kitchen Knight, Hand in Hand We'll Go,* and *Ghosts Go Haunting.* The double pages for the illustrations in Barbara Schiller's *The Kitchen Knight* are beautiful. They interpret well and with skillful simplicity the medieval chivalry and courtly love that is so much a part of the Arthurian legends. The texts and the illustrations in the other two books mentioned above could be used with great advantage to introduce Scottish dialect and lore to children from ages ten to fourteen years. Miss Hogrogian made handsome woodcut prints for the well-chosen poems written by Robert Burns that appear in *Hand in Hand We'll Go.* The touches of brown-and-yellowish green that are added to the key black figures, the backgrounds of gray, brown, and mustard yellow vividly evoke the prevailing mood and scene. Complementing qualities of humor, gentleness, and strength are revealed in Burns' poetry and in Nonny Hogrogian's prints. Also in the Scottish spirit are the illustrations for *Ghosts Go Haunting* by Sorche Nic Leodhas, (pseud. Alger Le Claire). The mood of the illustrations in this book is one of eeriness, although the element of humor is present, too. The collection of ghost tales (Scottish legends and ballads) is bewitching, and so are the illustrations that accompany them.

The woodcut prints by Antonio Frasconi are delightfully inventive. He is considered a master illustrator, and his work is frequently exhibited in the American Institute of Graphic Arts Children's Book Shows. He has written and illustrated several books. Some of his better-known titles are: *See Again, Say Again* which can be used to introduce foreign languages to children in grades three through seven; *The Snow and the Sun,* a South American folk rhyme in English and Spanish; and *The House that Jack Built,* a nursery rhyme in English and French. Frasconi's style in woodcut is bold and spirited with just the right touch of humor. He provides lively variety in line and color from book to book and from page to page. He usually uses bright colors, and each of the colors has its own independent shape. This helps to give his work an exceptionally vital composition. The title pages for each of his books are usually two-page spreads and are particularly striking. Hardly any young person who glanced at one would resist its invitation to read the book.

winter   inverno   **hiver**   **invierno**
wint'r   een-vehr'-noh   ee-vair'   een-v'yehr'-noh

skiing   **sledding**
skee'-ing   sled'-ding

sci   lo slittare
shee   loh sleet-tah'-reh

ski   **luge**
skee   lewzh

esquiismo   **ir en trineo**
es-kee-ees'-mo   eer en tree-nah'-yo

A Caldecott Medal winner for his illustrations in Barbara Emberley's *Drummer Hoff,* Ed Emberley handles the woodcut medium expertly. The pictures in *Drummer Hoff* were done in a thoroughly stylized manner as were the illustrations in Barbara Emberley's *One Wide River to Cross* and in his own *Green Says Go.* His lines are never careless, but he controls the wood medium with freedom and with ease. In *One Wide River to Cross,* the woodcuts are printed in black on solid-color backgrounds; the only exception is the rainbow page. Color prints are found in *Drummer Hoff* and *Green Says Go.* Although he used only three colors in these two books, he created the impression of thirteen colors by employing the overprinting technique. He made separate woodcuts for each of the three colors.

Mr. Emberley's colors are strong, bold, and flat, qualities which emphasize the simplified form that is so characteristic of this woodcut artist's work. While his woodcuts usually suit the contents and mood of the individual texts, each set of illustrations exemplifies his strong sense of design and his prolific imagination. Emberley's active sense of humor is expressed in his practice of exaggerating form and in his imaginative extension of subject matter. For example, there are the thoroughly stylized drawings of the basilisk, the unicorn, and the griffin in *One Wide River to Cross;* the charming but mammoth features of Paul Bunyan as seen in the double-page spreads in *The Story of Paul Bunyan;* and the pompous regalia worn by the military men in *Drummer Hoff.* His sense of humor, his vivid imaginative extension of the text, and his skill in handling the woodcut are very much apparent in these pictures as they are throughout any of his picture books.

Gil Miret made exquisite woodcuts for several children's books which are not children's picture books, however. His most striking woodcuts appear in Barbara C. Smucker's realistic fiction novel for children entitled *Wigwam in the City.* His lines are powerfully expressive, tending to choppy linear effects and to broad planes in bold black and white contrast. The tone of the drawings is as serious and real as the story itself.

Miret's work is different than Emberley's. When his work is compared with Emberley's illustrations (particularly those in *Drummer Hoff* and *One Wide River to Cross*), it is hard to believe that the same art medium was used by these two artists. The differences serve once again to remind us that each artist has his own unique style of drawing and of handling his art medium, and that each story will influence the mood expressed by use of line, detail, and tones.

Other woodcut artists abound, but space does not permit elaboration on their work. Two accomplished artists who cannot go unmentioned and who have contributed significantly to the field of children's literature are Ann Grifalconi who illustrated Mary Hays Weik's *The Jazz Man* and Elizabeth Bishop's *The Ballad of the Burglar of Babylon;* and Clement Hurd who made the unique illustrations that appear in *Wildfire* and *Wingfin and Topple,* both written by Evans G. Valens, Jr.

Cardboard Cutouts. Blair Lent uses laminated cardboard cutouts with watercolor overlays. His cutting tool is a single-edged razor blade. He has also used safety pins to create a particular effect in his prints. Mr. Lent used the cardboard cutouts to make the pictures for Margaret Hodges' *The Wave,* Ernest Small's *Baba Yaga,* and his own *Why the Sun and the Moon Are in the Sky,* and *John Tabor's Ride.*

Most of the stories he has illustrated are folktales and legends, and Blair Lent's pictures literally demand that the reader believe each highly fantastic tale. His art work matches the tone of each text. Through control of blade and brush, Lent leaves no doubt in the mind of the reader that a tidal wave can lift houses from the soil and carry them away, as was portrayed in *The Wave.* The pictures in *John Tabor's Ride* emphasize that the man who came to the whaler's rescue was spry and eccentric and that he wore an unruly beard that was speckled with sea-

Illustration by Blair Lent for THE WAVE by Margaret Hodges, adapted from Lafcadio Hearn's GLEANINGS IN BUDDHA-FIELDS. Pictures copyright © 1964 by Blair Lent. Reprinted with permission of Houghton Mifflin Company.

weed and tobacco. The reader is reassured by Lent's graphics in *Baba Yaga* that the witch is an old hag, frightening in appearance, but essentially harmless.

Lent uses free-flowing swirls in almost all of his books. His representations of wind, smoke, clouds, steam, or bodies of water are expressively moving and are drawn with grace and ease. Although all of his work is done with the blade and brush, he is able to depict a humorous overtone when and where it is the main mood, as it is in *John Tabor's Ride, Why the Sun and Moon Are in the Sky,* and *Baba Yaga.* When the mood is one of seriousness, and the feeling is one of tenseness, he can portray that, as he did so well in *The Wave* and *Oasis of the Stars,* the latter written by Olga Econamakis.

Linocut. An artist may select linoleum instead of wood to make a surface painting. Linoleum is more yielding than wood and thus, is an easier medium to handle. Because of its softness, gracefully curved lines can be cut, but the lines cannot be fine lines. Two types of linoleum may be used for linocuts, namely the kind which contains cork filler and permits clean-edged cuts, and the cork-free variety, the edge of which tends to crumble, thus causing the lines in a print to be slightly rough.

A skillfully contrived picture book illustrated by Marcia Brown with two-color linoleum cuts is *Dick Whittington and His Cat.* Her handling of this medium is vigorous and is nicely integrated with the concise and brief text (prose). The linocut prints in this book are suited to the period and the nature of this old favorite folktale. Much more dramatic are the handsome linocuts that illustrate the Hawaiian legend entitled *Backbone of the King; The Story of Paka'a and His Son Ku.* Once again, Marcia Brown vividly retains the authentic quality of the legend she has illustrated. In *Backbone of the King,* the exact features, the strong lines, and the effective use of color depict the fundamental struggles and powers of the ancient Hawaiians, as well as their frailties.

Wood Engraving. Wood engraving is a modification of the woodcut. For engraving, the wood must be cut across the trunk to obtain an end-grain. (In woodcuts, the side grain is used.) The most suitable wood

Illustration for BACKBONE OF THE KING; THE STORY OF PAKA'A AND HIS SON KU, written and illustrated by Marcia Brown. Copyright © 1966 by Marcia Brown. Reprinted with permission of Charles Scribner's Sons.

is boxwood, for it is the hardest, and it permits the engraver to cut fine curved lines in depth. The tool of the wood engraver is a burin similar to that used by a metal engraver. In contrast to a woodcut design, the wood engraving can carry considerable detail. It may also carry hatching in any direction and produce half tones.

The wood engravings that Philip Reed made for *Mother Goose and Nursery Rhymes* are done with considerable care and attention to detail, which is made possible and even encouraged by wood engraving as an illustrating technique. *Mother Goose and Nursery Rhymes* is a charming book, done in beautiful format, and Philip Reed has brought a refreshing interpretation to the popular as well as to the not-so-well-known rhymes. The human figures in his drawings appear to be rustic, and the animals are quite spirited. This wood engraver has revealed a delightfully droll sense of humor in his drawings. He uses a great deal of color in his work. *Mother Goose and Nursery Rhymes* was done in six colors, whereas three and four colors were used in Thurber's *Many Moons*.

Scratchboard. Scratchboard, also called scraperboard, is comparable to an etching. Scratchboard consists of a drawing board covered with smooth layers of chalk. The chalk layers are scraped with a sharp instrument (needle, graver, or blade) as is done when making an etching, in order to expose the underneath layer. The result is a precise, sharp line. Shading may be accomplished by parallel lines, crosshatching, or strippling. As with a wood engraving, the artist usually makes his drawing on tracing paper in the exact size that the illustration will be in the book. Then he transfers this onto the scartchboard "face up," and the drawing is inked in. After the ink has dried, he proceeds to scrape or scratch in his design. Scratchboard is primarily a black and white medium. When an artist uses this medium for illustrations in more than one color, he must employ the preseparated technique and make a separate scratchboard drawing for each color. Barbara Cooney is commonly associated with the scratchboard technique. Two other scratchboard artists worthy of attention are Leonard Everett Fisher and Anthony Ravielli. A brief discussion of their work follows.

Most notable of Barbara Cooney's illustrations are those that appear in *Chanticleer and the Fox*. Her work in this book, and in others, is recognized by her attention to minute detail. Each setting is authentically and faithfully presented, even to the carefully delineated thatch-roofed cottage and the variety of flowers that appear in the countryside scenes. The flowers and grasses in her drawings are typical of those that grew in the England of Chaucer's time. Miss Cooney even includes the magpie (which the people of Chaucer's day regarded as an evil omen) to

warn the reader of the disaster that is to befall Chanticleer. The delicacy
of the lines and the meticulous attention to detail highlight the medieval
flavor of this fable, and yet it is as fresh and contemporary as one would
want it to be. Barbara Cooney also expresses a sophisticated wit in her
drawings for this adaptation of *The Canterbury Tales*, and this spirit
prevails throughout her other picture books, too.

Leonard Everett Fisher used the scratchboard technique to make
the pictures for Ernest L. Thayer's *Casey at the Bat*, the famous poem

From CASEY AT THE BAT by Ernest
L. Thayer. Introduction by Casey
Stengel. Illustrated by Leonard Ever-
ett Fisher. Copyright © by Franklin
Watts, Inc. Reprinted with permission
of the publisher.

which first appeared in the *San Francisco Examiner*, June 3, 1888.
Fisher's pictorial version of this poem was selected in 1964 as one of that
year's "Ten Best Illustrated Children's Books." The illustrations are bold
black and white drawings, and are done in a style that is especially appealing to boys, a style that is masculine and well-disciplined.

Mr. Fisher also used scratchboard for the art work in the "Colonial
American Craftsmen" series, which includes *The Silversmiths, The Papermakers, The Hatters,* and *The Wigmakers.* The books in this series are
factual, and Leonard Everett Fisher's illustrations are filled with considerable detail. They reinforce the content of the text, but they also
extend it, and they help the reader to gain understanding and appreciation for the work and workers indigenous to colonial life. The illustra-

tions, which are strong and handsome black and white drawings, are an integral part of the books in this series. They are compatible with the brief, but interesting, descriptions of the techniques used by each colonial craftsman.

Mr. Fisher also used scratchboard to make the dramatic illustrations for Gerald W. Johnson's *America Is Born*. These drawings, which are fairly representational in style, vividly recreate the incidents involving the purchase of Manhattan Island by the colonial Dutch people from the American Indians.

Fisher's strikingly forceful scratchboard drawings also illustrate a book containing Abraham Lincoln's two most famous speeches, *The First Book Edition of the Gettysburg Address (and) The Second Inaugural*. These drawings emphasize Lincoln's most salient phrases. Other books in "The First Book Edition" series that Leonard Everett Fisher has illustrated profusely with very fine scratchboard drawings are those in which the complete text for each of the following documents or pieces of literature is given: The Declaration of Independence, John F. Kennedy's inaugural address, "A Man without a Country," "'A Message to Garcia,'" and the aforementioned "Casey at the Bat."

Anthony Ravielli used the scratchboard technique to make drawings for a science book series. The first book in this series is entitled *Wonders of the Human Body*. Another book in the series, *The World is Round*, is also illustrated with scratchboard drawings. Ravielli's illustrations are detailed and instructive. They are representational, and yet delightfully imaginative. Each set of illustrations is in perfect unity with the text, and each brings greater depth of understanding to the subject being considered.

Stone Lithography.   Stone lithography is a planographic technique for making a print. Few contemporary artists use this process, but among those who do are Lynd Ward, the D'Aulaires, and Felix Hoffmann.

The stone lithographer uses slabs of finegrained Bavarian limestone which are ground down and polished with Carborundum to produce a smooth and level surface. The artist then draws his design (laterally reversed) in litho drawing ink, using pen or brush. He may also use litho chalk or crayon to draw his design onto the stone slab. Whatever drawing material he uses to develop his subject on the stone, that material must be a compound of grease, wax, and lampblack. The grease mixture makes it possible to produce the printed image, and many copies of this image can be reproduced. The drawing must be the exact size as it will appear on the page in the book.

Having finished the drawing, the artist then proves the stone. The stone is treated with chemicals, gum arabic and nitric acid, and then a solution of asphalt in fatty oils. The oil sinks into the stone in the image areas or drawn parts; this area repels water. The undrawn areas protected by the gum arabic are water-sensitive and grease-resistant. At this point, the stone is dampened with water which soaks into the non-printing parts of the stone only. Next, a greasy ink is rolled over the stone. This ink is absorbed by the printing parts but repelled by the damp parts. Paper is pressed against the stone, and an impression is made from the inked (greased) areas. Upon close examination, the fine grain of the limestone can be discerned in the image that is impressed on the paper.

When more than one color is used, the artist must draw a separate design on another slab of stone. Only the part of the design that is to appear in a specific color is drawn on the stone. Thus, whatever elements in the picture that are to appear in red are drawn on one stone, the elements of the picture that contain blue are drawn on another stone, and so on, for each additional color. Eventually, the designs that appear on various stones are printed one after another on a single sheet of paper, and a multicolored lithoprint is created.

Examples of children's picture books illustrated in this technique are found in the classics that were written and illustrated by Edgar and Ingri D'Aulaire, specifically, *George Washington, Buffalo Bill, Pocahontas,* and *Abraham Lincoln.* (Recently, the D'Aulaires remade the illustrations for *Abraham Lincoln,* using acetates instead of the stone lithography technique, because the offset printers objected to handling the stone.) The colors used in their books are gay and bright. The full-page lithographs that appear in each of these books portray the greatness of each of the famous personages and help the reader to appreciate the contributions they made to America's history. The D'Aulaires have paid particular attention to details in their drawings, and each detail reflects the authenticity of these brief biographies. The interiors of the buildings, the clothing of the various periods, the actual appearance of the people about whom the biographies deal were depicted as authentically as the artists could possibly determine through careful research.

When illustrating fairy tales, Felix Hoffmann uses a considerable amount of color. *The Seven Ravens* was done in seven colors; five colors were used in the lithographs in *Rapunzel, The Sleeping Beauty,* and *The Wolf and the Seven Little Kids.* The illustrations for each of these fairy tales contribute much toward making each publication a handsome picture book. Each book will undoubtedly offer the young reader much pleasure, for the illustrations are works of art which are completely harmonious interpretations of the stories.

Mr. Hoffmann's figures are uniquely stylized. This artist gives careful attention to the features and facial expressions of each story character as well as to the articles of clothing worn by each. He pays particular attention to the settings and landscapes that surround the action so that the mood of each story is highlighted and sustained. It is through these interesting details that the young reader gets an exciting new look at his favorite old fairy tales.

Few artists have created such attractive interpretations of the traditional tales as has Felix Hoffmann. Considering that the medium Hoffmann used to create his colorful pictures was litho stone, his accomplishments are even more astonishing. He has also illustrated another book by using the prints made from stone lithograph. *Picture Bible* is done in black and white stone lithographs.

Lynd Ward is another important stone lithographic artist. He used this medium to make the drawings for May McNeer's *The Mexican Story* and *The Canadian Story*. Ward's work is characterized by its unique vitality and masculinity, and his approach to drawing appears to be one of sincerity and thoughtfulness. His lithographs evidence a disposition toward thoroughness and exactness. The scenes of Mexico and the wilds of Canada are detailed and are factually accurate, and yet they are not photographic. They are imaginative and are indigenous to the locale and the personalities he has portrayed. None of his illustrations is ever condescending. Instead, he tends to raise the viewer of his prints to greater heights of understanding and appreciation for the graphic arts, for good reading, and for the contents of the books they illustrate. Each book is filled with drawings that highlight the dramatic episodes and the pageantry that are so typical of May McNeer's stories. The realistic and detailed drawings are perfectly compatible with the texts they illustrate.

Color Separations (Acetate, Vellum, or Bourges). Many times, an artist will prepare his own color separations for his illustrations. Color separations are done with "overlays" of vellum, acetate, or Bourges.

Vellum is a heavy, translucent tracing paper that accepts all media—ink, pencil, paint, and crayon. Since it has a tendency to buckle if large areas are painted, and also because it stretches with changes in humidity, vellum may not be used where tight register is called for.

Acetate is more permanent than vellum; it is transparent and is available in several thicknesses. It will accept pencil, ink, or paint only if it is specially treated. When using acetate, the artist must make a separate drawing for each color. Regardless of the colors that will be included in the picture when it is printed, the artist uses black for each drawing.

Bourges is a series of transparent sheets which are coated with removable printing ink colors. To execute a color separation with Bourges, the artist removes, builds up, or cuts out sections of the color sheets. With Bourges, the artist can create color copy in separate color overlays. In fact, these colors can be used as color guides for the printer. This is not the case when acetates and vellum are used for copy, because the copy made with these media is in black. Color is achieved with ink on the press instead of in the preparation of the art work. The printer must use color swatches as his guide.

Following are the steps that are used to make color separations. The key drawing, which contains the plotting for the dominant color as well as for the major forms in the picture, is made first. Register marks, a cross drawn with the ruling pen, the T-square, and the triangle, are placed on the key drawing and each overlay sheet. One edge of the overlay is taped to the illustration board and is placed on top of the key drawing. The overlay is positioned so that each registration mark is perfectly alligned. The parts of the picture that are to be printed in the second color are drawn in black. This procedure is used with each additional color. The platemaker makes a separate plate for each color in the composition. The printer mixes his inks to match the color swatches that the artist has provided for each color in the combination.

This process is used by many contemporary book artists. Joan Walsh Anglund used pen-and-ink drawings with two-color overlays done on frosted acetate for the illustrations that appear in *A Friend Is Someone Who Likes You.* The D'Aulaires used acetates for their latest edition of *Abraham Lincoln.* They tried to make the prints look as though they had been done with stone lithography, the medium used to make the illustrations that appear in their biography series. They were successful, for only the keenest eye would notice that stone was not used to make these prints. Roger Duvoisin used acetate for the color separations in *Veronica* and *Petunia, Beware!,* two wonderfully humorous picture books for young readers.

H. A. Rey also does his own color separations. His key drawings are made with wash, india ink, and black crayon on drawing paper. The overlays are done in black and gray crayon, gray gouache, and flat Bourges grays on acetate.

Process Printing for Continuous Art Work. Continuous art work in full color, such as paintings and color montage, are reproduced by process color printing. The plates for process printing are made by the photomechanical separation of the primary colors—red, yellow, and blue. Black is added to reinforce the details and to facilitate the reproduction of neutral colors. Each plate is a complete halftone plate of one of the primary colors. The exact proportion and distribution of the color as it exists in the original subject is duplicated.

To make the color separation negatives for a set of four-color process plates, the full-color painting is photographed—once for each of the four component colors of the final full-color reproduction. Each photograph is made through a different filter which separates the particular color to be recorded. These color-separated negatives are in continuous tone. To make a halftone negative, the continuous tone negatives have to be re-photographed to produce continuous tone positives. Any color inaccuracies are corrected at this point. Then, the retouched positives are photographed through a halftone screen to create the four-color process halftone negatives. A separate printing plate is made for each color. Photomechanical separations are costly but are used occasionally. The camera was used to separate the colors that appear in the illustrations that were made by Beatrix Potter and Leslie Brooks. More recent art work which was prepared for color printing by camera were those done by Barbara Cooney in *A White Heron; A Story of Maine* and Brian Wildsmith's brilliant multicolored picture books.

Summary. Various painterly and graphic techniques are used by contemporary book artists. The artist may use pastels, watercolors, oil paints, pencil, crayon, tempera, gouache, or ink. He may make prints with woodcuts, wood engravings, linoleum cuts, scratchboard, stone lithography, and color separation media. The technique for reproducing continuous art work has been described. The artists' media and techniques have been discussed briefly, and some children's books which contain pictures made with one or more of these media or techniques have been identified.

SELECTED REFERENCES

ALIKI, (pseud. ALIKI BRANDENBERG). *A Weed Is a Flower, the Life of George Washington Carver.* Englewood Cliffs, N. J.: Prentice-Hall, Inc., 1965.

ANDERSEN, HANS CHRISTIAN. *Thumbelina.* Illustrated by Adrienne Adams. New York: Charles Scribner's Sons, 1961.

ANGLUND, JOAN WALSH. *A Friend Is Someone Who Likes You.* New York: Harcourt, Brace & World, Inc., 1958.

———. *In a Pumpkin Shell.* New York: Harcourt, Brace & World, Inc., 1960.

BISHOP, ELIZABETH. *The Ballad of the Burglar of Babylon.* Illustrated by Ann Grifalconi. New York: Farrar, Straus & Giroux, Inc., 1968.

BROWN, MARCIA. *Backbone of the King; The Story of Paka'a and His Son Ku.* New York: Charles Scribner's Sons, 1966.

———. *Dick Whittington and His Cat.* New York: Charles Scribner's Sons, 1950.

BROWN, MARGARET WISE. *The Golden Bunny.* Illustrated by Leonard Weisgard. New York: Golden Press, Inc., 1953.

BRYANT, SARA CONE. *The Burning Rice Fields*. Illustrated by Mamoru Funai. New York: Holt, Rinehart and Winston, Inc., 1963.

BURNS, ROBERT. *Hand in Hand We'll Go: Ten Poems*. Illustrated by Nonny Hogrogian. New York: Thomas Y. Crowell Company, 1965.

CHONZ, SELINA. *A Bell for Ursli*. Illustrated by Alois Carigiet. New York: Henry Z. Walck, Inc., 1953.

——. *Florina and the Wild Bird*. Illustrated by Alois Carigiet. New York: Henry Z. Walck, Inc., 1953.

——. *The Snowstorm*. Illustrated by Alois Carigiet. New York: Henry Z. Walck, Inc., 1958.

——NEY, BARBARA. *Chanticleer and the Fox*. New York: Thomas Y. Crowell Company, 1958.

——AULAIRE, EDGAR and INGRI. *Abraham Lincoln*. Garden City, N. Y.: Doubleday & Company, Inc., 1939.

——. *Buffalo Bill*. Garden City, N. Y.: Doubleday & Company, Inc., 1952.

——. *George Washington*. Garden City, N.Y.: Doubleday & Company, Inc., 1936.

——. *Pocahontas*, Garden City, N.Y.: Doubleday & Company, Inc., 1946.

DUVOISIN, ROGER A. *Veronica*. New York: Alfred A. Knopf, Inc., 1961.

——. *Petunia, Beware!* New York: Alfred A. Knopf, Inc., 1958.

ECONAMAKIS, OLGA. *Oasis of the Stars*. Illustrated by Blair Lent. New York: Coward-McCann, Inc., 1965.

EMBERLEY, BARBARA. *Drummer Hoff*. Illustrated by Ed Emberley. Englewood Cliffs, N.J.: Prentice-Hall, Inc., 1967.

——. *One Wide River to Cross*. Illustrated by Ed Emberley. Englewood Cliffs, N.J.: Prentice-Hall, Inc., 1966.

——. *The Story of Paul Bunyan*. Illustrated by Ed Emberley. Englewood Cliffs, N.J.: Prentice-Hall, Inc., 1963.

EMBERLEY, ED. *Green Says Go*. Illustrated by Ed Emberley. Boston: Little, Brown and Company, 1968.

First Book Edition of the Declaration of Independence, The. Illustrated by Leonard Everett Fisher. New York: Franklin Watts, Inc., 1968.

FISHER, LEONARD EVERETT. *The Hatters*. New York: Franklin Watts, Inc., 1965.

——. *The Papermakers*. New York: Franklin Watts, Inc., 1965.

——. *The Silversmiths*. New York: Franklin Watts, Inc., 1965.

——. *The Wigmakers*. New York: Franklin Watts, Inc., 1965.

FRANCOISE, (pseud. FRANCOISE SEIGNOBOSC). *Jeanne-Marie Counts Her Sheep*. New York: Charles Scribner's Sons, 1957.

——. *Noel for Jeanne-Marie*. New York: Charles Scribner's Sons, 1953.

——. *The Thank-You Book*. New York: Charles Scribner's Sons, 1947.

——. *The Things I Like*. New York: Charles Scribner's Sons, 1960.

FRASCONI, ANTONIO. *The House that Jack Built*. New York: Harcourt, Brace & World, Inc., 1958.

——. *See Again, Say Again*. New York: Harcourt, Brace & World, Inc., 1964.

——. *The Snow and the Sun*. New York: Harcourt, Brace & World, Inc., 1961.

GOUDEY, ALICE E. *The Day We Saw the Sun Come Up*. Illustrated by Adrienne Adams. New York: Charles Scribner's Sons, 1961.

——. *Houses from the Sea*. Illustrated by Adrienne Adams. New York: Charles Scribner's Sons, 1959.

GRAMATKY, HARDIE. *Bolivar.* New York: G. P. Putnam's Sons, 1961.

——. *Little Toot.* New York: G. P. Putnam's Sons, 1939.

GRIMM, JACOB and WILHELM. *Rapunzel.* Illustrated by Felix Hoffmann. New York: Harcourt, Brace & World, Inc., 1961.

——. *The Seven Ravens.* Illustrated by Felix Hoffmann. New York: Harcourt, Brace & World, Inc., 1963.

——. *The Shoemaker and the Elves.* Illustrated by Adrienne Adams. New York: Charles Scribner's Sons, 1960.

——. *The Wolf and the Seven Little Kids.* Illustrated by Felix Hoffmann. New York: Harcourt, Brace & World, Inc., n.d.

HADER, BERTA and ELMER. *The Big Snow.* New York: The Macmillan Company, 1948.

HALE, EDWARD EVERETT. *A Man without a Country.* Illustrated by Leonard Everett Fisher. New York: Franklin Watts, Inc., 1968.

HODGES, MARGARET. *The Wave.* Illustrated by Blair Lent. Boston: Houghton Mifflin Company, 1964.

HUBBARD, ELBERT. *A Message to Garcia.* Illustrated by Leonard Everett Fisher. New York: Franklin Watts, Inc., 1967.

JACOBS, JOSEPH, ed. "Tom Tit Tot" In *English Folk and Fairy Tales.* New York: G. P. Putnam's Sons, n.d.

JEWETT, SARAH ORNE. *A White Heron; a Story of Maine.* Illustrated by Barbara Cooney. New York: Thomas Y. Crowell Company, 1963.

JOHNSON, GERALD W. *America is Born.* Illustrated by Leonard Everett Fisher. New York: William Morrow & Co., Inc., 1958.

KENNEDY, JOHN F. *The First Book Edition of John F. Kennedy's Inaugural Address; Proclamation by Lyndon B. Johnson.* Illustrated by Leonard Everett Fisher. New York: Franklin Watts, Inc., 1964.

LAWRENCE, JACOB. *Harriet and the Promised Land.* New York: Windmill Books, Inc./Simon & Schuster, Inc., 1968.

LENT, BLAIR. *John Tabor's Ride.* Boston: Atlantic Monthly Press, 1966.

——. *Why the Sun and the Moon Are in the Sky.* Boston: Houghton Mifflin Company, 1968.

LINCOLN, ABRAHAM. *The First Book Edition of the Gettysburg Address, (and) The Second Inaugural.* Illustrated by Leonard Everett Fisher. New York: Franklin Watts, Inc., 1963.

McCLOSKEY, ROBERT. *Time of Wonder.* New York: The Viking Press, Inc., 1957.

MacDONALD, GOLDEN. *The Little Island.* Illustrated by Leonard Weisgard. Garden City, N.Y.: Doubleday & Company, Inc., 1946.

McNEER, MAY. *The Canadian Story.* Illustrated by Lynd Ward. New York: Farrar, Straus & Giroux, Inc., 1958.

——. *The Mexican Story.* Illustrated by Lynd Ward. New York: Farrar, Straus & Giroux, Inc., 1953.

MUNARI, BRUNO. *The Birthday Present.* Cleveland: The World Publishing Company, 1959.

——. *Bruno Munari's ABC.* Cleveland: The World Publishing Company, 1960.

——. *Who's There? Open the Door!* Cleveland: The World Publishing Company, 1957.

——. *Bruno Munari's Zoo.* Cleveland: The World Publishing Company, 1963.

Ness, Evaline. *Double Discovery*. New York: Charles Scribner's Sons, 1965.
———. *Josephina February*. New York: Charles Scribner's Sons, 1963.
———. *Tom Tit Tot*. New York: Charles Scribner's Sons, 1965.
Nic Leodhas, Sorche. (pseud. Alger LeClaire). *Always Room for One More*. Illustrated by Nonny Hogrogian. New York: Holt, Rinehart & Winston, Inc., 1965.
———. *Ghosts Go Haunting*. Illustrated by Nonny Hogrogian. New York: Holt Rinehart & Winston, Inc., 1965.
Perrault, Charles. *The Sleeping Beauty*. Illustrated by Felix Hoffmann. New York: Harcourt, Brace & World, Inc., 1959.
Piatti, Celestino. *Celestino Piatti's Animal ABC*. New York: Atheneum Publishers, 1966.
———. *The Happy Owls*. New York: Atheneum Publishers, 1964.
Politi, Leo. *Juanita*. New York: Charles Scribner's Sons, 1958.
———. *Little Leo*. New York: Charles Scribner's Sons, 1951.
———. *Pedro, the Angel of Olvera Street*. New York: Charles Scribner's Sons, 1946.
———. *Saint Francis and the Animals*. New York: Charles Scribner's Sons, 1959.
———. *Song of the Swallows*. New York: Charles Scribner's Sons, 1949.
Ravielli, Anthony. *Wonders of the Human Body*. New York: The Viking Press, Inc., 1954.
———. *The World Is Round*. New York: The Viking Press, Inc., 1963.
Reed, Philip. ed. *Mother Goose and Nursery Rhymes*. New York: Atheneum Publishers, 1963.
Robbins, Ruth. *Baboushka and the Three Kings*. Illustrated by Nicolas Sidjakov. Berkeley: Parnassus Press, 1960.
Scheer, Julian. *Rain Makes Applesauce*. Illustrated by Marvin Bileck. New York: Holiday House, Inc., 1964.
Schiller, Barbara. *The Kitchen Knight*. Illustrated by Nonny Hogrogian. New York: Holt, Rinehart & Winston, Inc., 1965.
Sendak, Maurice. *Where the Wild Things Are*. New York: Harper & Row, Publishers, 1963.
Small, Ernest. *Baba Yaga*. Illustrated by Blair Lent. Boston: Houghton Mifflin Company, 1966.
Smucker, Barbara C. *Wigwam in the City*. Illustrated by Gil Miret. New York: E. P. Dutton & Co., Inc., 1966.
Tennyson, Alfred Lord. *The Charge of the Light Brigade*. Illustrated by Alice and Martin Provensen. New York: Golden Press, Inc., 1964.
Thayer, Ernest L. *The First Book Edition of Casey at the Bat*. Illustrated by Leonard Everett Fisher. New York: Franklin Watts, Inc., 1964.
Thurber, James. *Many Moons*. Illustrated by Louis Slobodkin. New York: Harcourt, Brace & World, Inc., 1943.
Tresselt, Alvin. *Hide and Seek Fog*. Illustrated by Roger Duvoisin. New York: Lothrop, Lee & Shepard Co., Inc., 1965.
Tudor, Tasha. *A Is for Annabelle*. New York: Henry Z. Walck, Inc., 1954.
———. *Around the Year*. New York: Henry Z. Walck, Inc., 1957.
———. *Linsey Woolsey*. New York: Henry Z. Walck, Inc., 1946.
———. *1 Is One*. New York: Henry Z. Walck, Inc., 1956.
———. *Pumpkin Moonshine*. New York: Henry Z. Walck, Inc., 1962.

VALENS, EVANS G., JR. *Wildfire.* Illustrated by Clement Hurd. Cleveland: The World Publishing Company, 1963.

————. *Wingfin and Topple.* Illustrated by Clement Hurd. Cleveland: The World Publishing Company, 1962.

VON JÜCHEN, AUREL. *The Holy Night.* Illustrated by Celestino Piatti. New York: Atheneum Publishers, Inc., 1968.

WEIK, MARY HAYS. *The Jazz Man.* Illustrated by Ann Grifalconi. New York: Atheneum Publishers, 1966.

WILDSMITH, BRIAN. *Brian Wildsmith's Birds.* New York: Franklin Watts, Inc., 1967.

chapter 4

using illustrations in the school

One of the most effective ways to stimulate learning is to surround children with attractive books about things of interest to them. They should be exposed to these books during their preschool years and throughout their entire school careers. A balanced collection in a school library includes many books that satisfy varied reading interests and that span a wide range of reading difficulties. Chances are very good that students will acquire habits of independent reading, study, and learning that will endure throughout their lifetime when they are encouraged to explore the book collection, to pursue their own interests, to read as widely and deeply as they will.[1]

Illustrated books are much preferred by children. An astute and ambitious book selector will be able to find quantities of illustrated books that would meet the varied reading interests and reading achievement levels of most children in any one classroom. Picture books are not written only for the preschoolers or for kindergarten—primary school children. There are numerous picture books that would delight students in the upper grades and in high school, and even the adult.

One can find very fine picture books about a wide variety of topics addressed to readers of all ages and of various levels of reading achievements. Examination of the books which, because of the excellent illustrations each contained, have been included in the American Institute of Graphic Arts Children's Book Shows, will reveal the many topics on which picture books are focused. The American Indian, animals of all kinds, history of the United States, explorers, biographies of interesting and important people, modes of transportation of the present and of the past, religion, wars, number books and alphabet books, the circus, fish

---

[1]James Cass, ed. *Books in the Schools.* (New York: American Book Publishers Council, 1961), p. iii.

and fishing, atoms, astronomy, and space travel are a mere sampling of the topics about which picture books are written. The list is unending. Think of the wonderful variety of books that one can offer readers both young and old when one considers the *illustrated books,* the broader classification of books which contain pictures and text. A reader of any age could be given beautifully illustrated books about almost any subject; he could use illustrated books to learn or to escape, or to have fun and pleasure from his reading.

Reading is a process which demands that the reader understand the printed word. It is a process which encourages the reader to identify with the book characters and with the action of the story. It is a process which can provide the reader with a wealth of vicarious experiences. Illustrations in books can help the reader to create visual images and can help him to go beyond the printed word. Illustrations in books can facilitate the reader's comprehension, identification, and experiencing.

The youngest as well as the oldest child can gain considerable fun and pleasure from reading an attractively illustrated and well-written book. He can use reading as a wholesome means of escape from a life that for him may be humdrum and provincial, or which may be filled with pressures and grimness. He can use books as a source from which to gain increased knowledge and understanding of himself and others and of the world in which he lives. Acquiring knowledge and understanding often brings considerable pleasure and stimulation to the reader. To some degree, certain developmental needs can be satisfied through reading because the reader identifies with the book characters and the action of the story. Thus he can experience life vicariously and satisfy basic and developmental needs.

Since illustrations help to make the printed word more concrete and to extend the text, it follows that an illustrated book could help the reader to realize fun, pleasure, and varied worthwhile experiences more completely. Picture books and other illustrated books can help educators to accomplish even more, however. In the pages that follow, some specific objectives will be identified, objectives that can be realized when illustrated books (especially picture books) are chosen with care and are used "the right way with the right child at the right time."

A Source of Pleasure. Reading just for the enjoyment it brings should be encouraged at all levels in the educational program. It should be recognized as a perfectly respectable and rewarding activity. When a book is well-chosen in terms of content and style of illustrations, the reader is likely to become thoroughly involved in it and to get a feeling of exhilaration and well-being. This gift of pleasure-filled hours can come from selective reading of beautifully illustrated books of fiction or non-fiction, prose or poetry, classical literary selections or contemporary works, fantasy or realistic stories, humorous tales or serious narratives.

Occasionally, the child will want to read and examine a factual picture book like *Houses from the Sea* and *Butterfly Time*, semi-narratives by Alice E. Goudey. Both of these books are simple texts with attractive representational pictures in exquisite colors done by Adrienne Adams. Each of these picture books should alert the reader to the wonder and beauty that surround him. In *Houses from the Sea*, the rhythmic text which contains the common names of a variety of seashells, and the carefully detailed full-color illustrations would fascinate many young readers. The accurately colored drawings of twelve common butterflies and the explanation of the life cycle of butterflies would also bring considerable pleasure to the young reader of *Butterfly Time*.

Children like to read factual books that are profusely and attractively illustrated. There is no question but that they can gain much pleasure from books that have a factual slant. One need only watch the expressions on the faces of children of any age as they sit in the school library or in their own classrooms, reading or just looking at factual picture books. Their expressions are those of awe and engrossed attention when the factual books deal with topics of interest to them. There is much pleasure to be had, indeed, a great feeling of well-being and accomplishment is experienced when one finishes reading or examining an interesting factual book or story book.

Individuals vary in their reading interests. What brings pleasure and enjoyment to one reader may not bring pleasure and enjoyment to another. Individuals vary considerably, too, in their responses to the illustrations that accompany stories. One child may be delighted with *The Nightingale*, translated by Eva Le Gallienne, and illustrated by Nancy Ekholm Burkert with stunning double-page color paintings and decorations that are suggestive of early Chinese screens. Another child, of the same age, may get far more enjoyment from the more sophisticated fantasy by Randall Jarrell entitled *The Bat Poet*, which is sparsely illustrated with Maurice Sendak's exquisite black and white line drawings that look like fine etchings. A young male reader may find that the realistic illustrations in Lynd Ward's *The Biggest Bear* and the main character's repeatedly unsuccessful attempts to get rid of his beloved pet constitute a thoroughly enjoyable book. This same boy might be unable to appreciate either Alice Dalgliesh's lengthy and tension-filled adventure story, *The Bears on Hemlock Mountain*, or Helen Sewell's highly stylized

Illustration by Nancy Ekholm Burkert for THE NIGHTINGALE by H. C. Anderson, translated by Eva Le Gallienne. Pictures copyright © 1965 by Nancy Ekholm Burkert. Reprinted with permission from Harper & Row, Publishers, Inc.

illustrations that accompany it; whereas both the story and the illustrations of *The Bears on Hemlock Mountain* might delight another boy in his class.

Some picture books are fairly universal in their appeal and will bring many pleasure-filled hours to almost any reader. An example is the picture book entitled *Mop Top*, a slapstick account of what happened to a little boy who would not get his hair cut. The hero of this story has red hair, and Don Freeman's humorous line drawings highlight this fact. The use of red with the line drawings adds splash to the book and will attract a child's attention. Whether red haired, blond, or brunette, most children will find it an absolute delight.

Few children will fail to appreciate the efforts of Peter as he struggles in his attempt to learn to whistle, as depicted in Ezra Jack Keats' picture book *Whistle for Willie*, another book with general appeal. The illustrations are done in collage and paint, and they stress the universality of a child's struggle to accomplish the adult feat of whistling.

Narrative verse is the form of literature that Aileen Fisher used in her picture book, *In the Middle of the Night,* to report what happens at nighttime to the small creatures that inhabit the woods, grass, and sky. Adrienne Adams' illustrations add considerable charm to this book and serve to emphasize Miss Fisher's reassuring message that the wonder and beauty which fills the night leave little room for fears.

Joyous hours will be given the child who has a chance to hear the story and see the illustrations in *One Morning in Maine.* Robert McCloskey's text and illustrations almost demand repeated perusal by five-or-six-year-olds who will most certainly agree with Sal that it is a wonderfully important occasion when one loses his first tooth. Both the storyline and the realistic illustrations in *One Morning in Maine* serve as a comforting reminder to the young reader that he is growing up, just like Sal and his friends.

A Source for Fun and Laughter. Picture books and other illustrated books can be used to bring smiles and laughter to youngsters. The capacity for enjoying humor and nonsense can be fostered through stories and through the illustrations that accompany them. Much of the child's world—in school and out—is filled with pressures and grimness, or at least, with serious and matter-of-fact realities. It is important that he have fun and laughter in order to relieve tensions caused by these pressures and realities. It is important that he be allowed to forget his problems, even temporarily, so that he can view them in proper perspective, perhaps, or reinforce himself with sufficient emotional fortitude so that he can cope with his problems, or hopefully, resolve them eventually.

Humor for young children must be simple and spontaneous. Most children chuckle at Don Freeman's *Dandelion*, the story of a lion who dresses up so much for a party that his hostess fails to recognize him and refuses to let him in. The story and the cartoon-style illustrations are indeed humorous, and yet the theme, that one should be true to one's nature, comes out "loud and clear." Since it is presented in this delightfully humorous manner rather than in a didactic manner, the young reader is more likely to accept this message as being a worthy one.

Many times, laughter is provoked when the unexpected occurs. The simply-written, repetitious story of *Just Like Everyone Else* by Karla Kuskin has a surprise ending that delights children. Jonathan James does what everyone else does. He gets up in the morning, gets dressed, eats breakfast, and says goodbye to his family. Then, to everyone's surprise, Jonathan James flies off to school! Mrs. Kuskin's simple line drawings which illustrate this little picture book are perfectly compatible with the relatively naive and unelaborate story. This book offers fun purely for the sake of fun and is a fine book to have in a book collection for very young readers.

The surprise ending, as well as the peddler's frustration at his inability to get his caps back from the monkeys, provide the bases for the humor in the old favorite, *Caps for Sale*, that was written and illustrated by Esphyr Slobodkina. This story was written in traditional folktale style and was appropriately illustrated with simple line drawings and bold opaque colors. Children enjoy dramatizing this simple tale. They have no difficulty playing the role of the angry peddler who vainly tries to convince the monkeys that his caps must be returned, and they have much fun portraying the mimicking, mischievous monkeys.

The impact that Dr. Seuss, (pseud. Theodore S. Geisel) has had on helping children to appreciate simple satirical humor is well-known. Exaggeration, incongruity, and the discomfiture of others are depicted in text and cartoon-style illustrations in the story, *Horton Hatches the Egg*. The situations, plus wonderful play on words, provide the humor for this narrative poem about Horton, the elephant who kept his word—one hundred percent! As a humorist (satirist perhaps is a better word for his brand of humor), Dr. Seuss has written and illustrated several other narratives that have provoked gales of laughter from young readers. His means of creating highly amusing situations are usually the same. Among his fantastic tales in picture book format that children find humorous are *And to Think that I Saw It on Mulberry Street, The 500 Hats of Bartholomew Cubbins, The King's Stilts,* and *The Cat in the Hat.* Few children will fail to see some humor in his stories, especially if they can view the illustrations while the text is being read to them. Nonetheless, a five-or-six-year-old child who is fairly immature, or who is lacking in a rich background of experience, may miss Dr. Seuss' clever verbal wit and will likely fail to appreciate fully the humor and satire of the situations portrayed in each narrative.

Like Dr. Seuss, Tomi Ungerer presents a rather sophisticated humor in his writing and illustrating of children's picture books. Especially worthy of note are *Moon Man* and *Zeralda's Ogre. Moon Man* is a cleverly imaginative tale which relates the series of events that happen to the Moon Man after he descends to Earth on the fiery tale of a comet. He is thought to be an invader and is captured and thrown into prison. By means of unique lunar powers, he escapes and has a gay time for a short while but eventually returns to the moon by way of a space craft. *Zeralda's Ogre* is about a child-eating ogre whose food preferences undergo change during the course of the story. The conversations about such culinary creations as roast turkey á la Cinderella and chocolate sauce Rasputin provoke much of the humor in this picture book. Both stories are illustrated with bold cartoon-type illustrations that effectively capture their humorous qualities. Vivid colors are used in both books. If a child had sufficient background of knowledge and experience (phases of the moon, space craft, and common folktales), these imaginative stories would bring him many moments of fun and laughter.

The fun derived from reading *The Loudest Noise in the World* by Benjamin Elkin comes partly from the closeness to real life situations and the humorous exaggeration of these situations portrayed by the author, but James Daugherty's vigorous illustrations make this story of a little boy's reaction to his grandfather's snoring even funnier.

The nonsense in *The Scroobious Pip* demands that the reader have an active imagination. He must go far beyond his "real" world to find humor in the absolutely non-existent, 'way out creatures and situations that are described in this nonsense poem which was begun by Edward Lear and finished by Ogden Nash. If the reader is a creative thinker, he probably could appreciate the nonsensical quality of this poem without really needing the illustrations that accompany the text. On the other hand, Nancy Burkert's detailed illustrations would be especially helpful to those readers who have not as yet been introduced to Lear's brand of humor and who have not learned to be free and imaginative in their response to his literary masterpieces.

Four-and-five-year-olds are thrilled with the loveable, but horribly ugly monsters that Max meets in his dreams as portrayed by Maurice Sendak in *Where the Wild Things Are*. The appearance of the monsters and their "wild rumpus" create an eerie atmosphere, and yet the monsters' happy expressions and Max's power over the animals can't help but cause the reader to chuckle. Most children thoroughly enjoy having *Where the Wild Things Are* read to them, and they spend much time examining each fantastic creature that was created by Sendak's active imagination. The author has used an interesting technique to involve the reader in Max's fantasies. As Max moves into his fanciful world, the pages become increasingly filled with color. As he moves back again into his real world, more white space fills the pages. In all probability, young readers will not be conscious of the manipulative use of color. Nonetheless, the impact of the technique will be felt. The readers, like Max, will move into the fanciful world and then back again to reality.

Seeing Oneself as a Functioning, Growing Individual.   Literature may be used to help children realize that growing up is a universal human experience. This very process of growing up is not an easy one, and contemporary literature does depict this truism. Books permit a young reader to view and to experience (vicariously) many of the realities of growing up; they permit the reader to "try out" various roles and acts of living so that he may eventually select the ones that are most suitable to his unique needs and personality makeup. Perhaps the picture books which are discussed in the following paragraphs serve to justify a growing conviction that books can be used to help children understand that they are growing, functioning individuals, similar to other people in some ways, and also different from people in other ways.

A long-time favorite with four-, five-, and six-year-olds is *The Growing Story* which was written by Ruth Krauss. The text, and the precise but simple line drawings by Phyllis Rowand, depict a little boy watching many things grow—grass, flowers, chickens, and a puppy, among other things. He doesn't realize until he puts on his warm clothes in late autumn that he, too, has grown. Identification with the book character who is involved in a situation as common as this will be easy for the young reader. He will appreciate more fully that he, too, is growing up. *The Growing Story* can be used to help the young reader accept with ease and grace the physical changes that are taking place within him.

An Anteater Named Arthur by Bernard Waber is a fantasy. None-theless, the young reader will easily see himself in this endearing and exasperating creature. The reader of *An Anteater Named Arthur* will find comfort in learning that other children (even a young anteater) can be forgetful, messy, inquisitive, choosy, and loveable. The humor in the text is simple and obvious. Bernard Waber's droll cartoon-style illus-trations are, for the most part, in pink and brown, and they help to make this a thoroughly engaging picture book. They also help the child to laugh at himself and perhaps, even to view life in a more relaxed and wholesome manner.

Many children desperately want a dog or some other pet. These children will understand and identify with the charming little girl in *What Mary Jo Wanted* by Janice Udry. Mary Jo experiences trials and tribulations in order to get a puppy. And then she must accomodate the pet to her family. Pleasant and simple sketches were made by Eleanor Mill to illustrate this picture book. They support the warm and affec-tionate spirit that prevails throughout the story.

From his first junior book on, the young reader can use books to find out something of what people, including himself, are really like. Whether or not he has actually met with poverty or with tenement living, whether or not he has observed family strife and quarreling, picture books like *Striped Ice Cream* by Joan Lexau and *The Jazz Man* by Mary Hays Weik will help him to have a better understanding of basic human emotions and human frailties. The free pencil sketches that John Wilson made to illustrate *Striped Ice Cream* emphasize the genuine family situa-tions that are portrayed in this engaging story. The problems of poverty experienced by this self-reliant, fatherless Negro family are a major part of Joan Lexau's realistic story. An equally important aspect of the story is the believable behavior of the five children in the family. Young readers from every social and cultural group will recognize the universal human traits that are delineated in *Striped Ice Cream*. There is little doubt that they will identify with the ups and downs, the quarreling and subsequent making up of this interesting family. The story of *The Jazz Man* is direct and true, strong and honest. The hunger and the family conflict, as well as the family's closeness to each other are included be-cause they are all a part of life the author writes about. *The Jazz Man* may be a grim story, but it is not depressing or fatalistic. The text is full of beautiful imagery, and the superb woodcut illustrations by Ann Grifal-coni open windows to the world. Through these windows, children will see more and more each time they read *The Jazz Man*.

Another book which highlights aspects of family life is *Every Day a Dragon*, written by Joan Lexau. This mirthful story about a daily game

of make-believe between a little boy and his father will add to the
reader's feeling of well-being. Ben Shecter's sketches are very appropriate for this amusing picture book.

These are only a few of the books which exemplify the fact that
picture books and illustrated books can be used to help children of all
ages realize that their wishes, feelings, and actions may be very normal,
that oftentimes they are merely a part of the process of growing up.
Books such as these may also be used to help children recognize that
people differ in their needs and wishes and feelings, and these differences
should be cherished.

Vocabulary and Concept Builders. An illustrated book, especially
a picture book, is a construction in language and in art, both of which are
modes of symbolic representation of the concrete world and of human
experiences. When the writer and the illustrator express these representations in ways that permit the reader to create accurate and detailed
images of his own, and to relate new or extended meanings to old
associations, the result is that the reader will grow in language power;
he will form more mature and more adequate concepts about himself and
his gradually increasing world.

Actually, wide reading and close reading of all forms of literature
will help the child grow in word power and will help him to view his

world more adequately and accurately. However, if a child comes to school with limited language facility and with an impoverished experiential background, it is best that he read many picture story books about his here-and-now world, as well as "concept" books, both of which will help him learn to make generalizations and to extend his vocabulary.

Some of the books included in the series entitled *Let's-Read-and-Find-Out* are excellent for this purpose. The titles are self-explanatory, but it might be well to say that, in each case, the child is alerted to his immediate surroundings and is encouraged to look, feel, smell, and listen carefully. His curiosity is aroused, and he is helped to be more responsive to all kinds of experiences. Some of the titles in this series are *Follow Your Nose* and *Look at Your Eyes*, both of which were written by Paul Showers and illustrated by Paul Galdone; *My Five Senses* and *My Hands*, which were written and illustrated by Aliki.

Other picture books that are effective vocabulary and concept builders include the *"Noisy Books,"* written by Margaret Wise Brown.

The Country Noisy Book, illustrated by Leonard Weisgard, portrays the sounds made by country animals, whereas *Goodnight Moon,* also written by Margaret Wise Brown, but illustrated by Clement Hurd, identifies the many noises one hears in the dark and explains what the more common creatures do when it is dark. Another book which explains nighttime happenings is *While Susie Sleeps,* a matter-of-fact interpretation by Nina Schneider, the author, and Dagmar Wilson, the illustrator.

Two simple little picture books, one which presents the names given to the young of some common animals, and the other which tells of the foods eaten by certain animals, are *Where's My Baby* and *Feed the Animals,* both of which were written and illustrated by Hans A. Rey.

Brian Wildsmith's books on groupings of birds, wild animals, and fishes appeal to the more sophisticated children; his fantasy-colored creatures would certainly stimulate their imaginations. The combination of these unusual pictures and the terms which are used to assemble each of the groups are excellent vocabulary builders. When grouping the birds, captions like the following are used: "a sedge of herons," "a nye of pheasants," and "a stare of owls." The groupings of wild animals include "a skulk of foxes" and "a pride of lions." To mention a few of the groupings of fishes, there are "a cluster of porcupine fish," "a flock of dolphins," "a battery of barracuda," and "a flotilla of swordfish." Brian Wildsmith's nimble brush and his choice of words should contribute much toward enriching the reading, speaking, and writing vocabularies of those who read and examine his books carefully.

Extending Background of Experiences. It is important that the child's world extend beyond himself and his home. He must be introduced to a greater world, a more varied world. This can be done, of course, through real and actual experiences, but picture books may be used to extend the child's world, too. Rich experiences, be they real or vicarious, will permit the child to function as an effective citizen in a cosmopolitan and vital world. A rich background of experiences is essential if the child is to realize success and is to attain more realistically his actual potential in the academic world. Children have an inner drive and desire for knowledge and intellectual stimulation. Numerous carefully chosen books can provide the young learners with enriching vicarious experiences. Books that are adequately illustrated can be an excellent source from which to obtain a wealth of information in a clear and meaningful way.

Alert, inquisitive young minds will find some interesting and satisfying answers about the wondrous world of nature that are provided in Betty Jean Lifton's picture book, *The Secret Seller.* An effective combination of black and white photographs and stylized illustrations in four colors is used to tell the story of Ken, a little boy who lives in an apartment building in New York City. The youngster has everything he wants except a secret. In his encounters with several other children, it develops that each child has a secret that he will not share with Ken. This portion of the narrative is told by means of black and white photographs. The many secrets that Ken finds in Central Park, with the aid of the secret seller, are portrayed with four-color illustrations. Where squirrels store their nuts, how bees gather nectar from the flowers, where ants store their food and raise their young, are a few of the many secrets that are brought to Ken's attention. *The Secret Seller* is an irresistible story, told with the intent to make children more curious about their surroundings.

Some things about color that children would like to know—the names of colors, what happens when colors are mixed, and how colors "talk" or affect moods and feelings—may be learned from *Green Says Go,* a simple picture book, written and illustrated by Ed Emberley. The illustrations are woodcut prints in bright, bold colors and are imaginative and witty. This brief and simple concept book is noteworthy in that it stimulates the average child to be more sensitive to the varied uses of color and encourages him to experiment with painting so that he can make his own unusual colors and shades.

Much about the life patterns of wild animals, especially their struggle for survival, can be learned from *The Barn,* a picture book that was written and illustrated by John Schoenherr. The black and white illustrations are "subjectively respresentational." Along with the text, they portray with sympathetic realism the stark terror experienced by the skunk when he becomes the prey of a great horned owl during a severe summer drought. John Schoenherr tells with expressive words and illustrations a grim and moving story that is sure to enlighten many young readers.

Ranked among the most beautiful books ever published are the longtime favorites created by Holling C. Holling. Each of these books follows the same design and format. Numerous large, strikingly dramatic colored illustrations done by Mr. Holling are found in each book. Marginal drawings and diagrams elaborate on significant details mentioned or implied in the brief but highly informative texts. A wealth of knowledge can be obtained from these superb books. In *Minn of the Mississippi* and *Pagoo,* the life histories of a turtle and a crawfish, respectively, are traced. A map is provided for the reader's use in following the travels of a small canoe as narrated in *Paddle-to-the-Sea.* The reader will learn much about geography, particularly about the regions of the Great Lakes, Niagara Falls, the St. Lawrence River, and the Grand Banks off the coast of Newfoundland. A reference map is also included in *Tree in the Trail* to help bring to the reader a greater insight into the various aspects of the westward movement. This story, which tells of the incidents that happened under and around one particular tree that stood on the westward trail, reveals facts that relate directly to subject disciplines such as anthropology, history, and geography. *Seabird* is a story about the triumphs in navigation. More specifically, it is an exciting adventure story revolving around Seabird, an ivory gull, through whose eyes the reader learns about whaling ships, clipper ships, steamships, and aircraft. The author took three or four years to write each book, because his narratives, paintings, and sketches were based upon the findings of his painstaking and conscientious research. Each book would make a fine contribution to any child's personal library.

The course of a forest fire caused by a flash of lightning is depicted with fascinating imagery and suspense in *Wildfire* which was written by Evans G. Valens, Jr. and illustrated by Clement Hurd. How the birds and animals of the forest react to the raging fire, and how the cycle of life is resumed in the burned-out area are told in prose that reads like exquisite verse. The striking illustrations in this large picture book were made with a print-on-print technique. That is, Clement Hurd, the illustrator, placed linoleum block prints on a background of print made from the grain of weathered wood, after which the prints were made on wet rice paper.

One need not use only the here-and-now picture story book or an informational book to introduce the young reader to a more spacious and varied world. The point of view of dolls, of talking animals, of animated engines, or of buildings can give piquancy to small adventures. There are the simple little picture books that Russell Hoban created about a lovable badger named Frances who, in *Bedtime for Frances*, comes up with clever reasons for staying up past her bedtime, or in *A Baby Sister for Frances*, demonstrates her importance when she is "blessed" with a new baby sister.

The house that Virginia Lee Burton created in *The Little House* comes alive, and over the years, experiences the inevitable changes that are the result of progress. These books and numerous others present, through appropriate language and illustrations, meaningful commentaries upon experiences common to most children. Reading about these experiences brings satisfaction to the children for it permits them to look back at experiences which they have had, or to share and look back at experiences which they have not had but which the writers or other people have had.[2]

Providing a Literary and Cultural Heritage. Several popular imaginative literary selections that have been enjoyed by children for generations have recently been illustrated by some of the most outstanding contemporary book artists. Among them are Margot Zemach, Uri Shulevitz, Ezra Jack Keats, Adrienne Adams, Evaline Ness, and Paul Nussbaumer.

Margot Zemach has illustrated a number of folk classics that are representative of several national or regional groups. She made the line drawings for *Mommy, Buy Me a China Doll* (retold by Harve Zemach), a picture book version of an Ozark Mountain area folk song. She has also illustrated several Russian folk pieces. Among these are *Salt* (retold by Harve Zemach), the story of Ivan, the foolish son of a Russian merchant, who brings salt to his homeland when his older and supposedly wiser brothers fail in this task; and *The Speckled Hen* (retold by Harve Zemach), an amusing Russian nursery rhyme that tells of the disturbances caused by a hen that lays a speckled egg. Margot Zemach also illustrated *Nail Soup* (retold by Harve Zemach), the somewhat altered Swedish version of the tale about soldiers who make soup with nails. In each of the books mentioned here, Margot Zemach's illustrations are strong, rustic line drawings and are in full-color wash.

Uri Shulevitz won the 1969 Caldecott Medal for his illustrations of a Russian folktale entitled *The Fool of the World and the Flying Ship*, by Arthur Ransome. He also illustrated the Hebrew legend, *The Carpet of Solomon,* (retold by Sulamith Ish-Kishor). The pictures in this book match so well the dramatic account of the proud King Solomon and how he learns the wisdom of humility. Shulevitz's line and wash drawings are quite different from those done by Margot Zemach. And yet, they seem equally appropriate for the tales they interpret.

Another folktale in picture book form and worthy of note is *John Henry*, retold and illustrated by Ezra Jack Keats. This American legend is illustrated in the modern art style associated with Keats. Nonetheless, the large, bold figures reflect the spirit of the powerful legendary figure who was "born with a hammer in his hand."

Adrienne Adams illustrated the Grimm Brothers' fairytale, *The Shoemaker and the Elves*, with soft watercolors. Evaline Ness used woodcuts to make the brown, blue, and black prints for *Tom Tit Tot*, a variant of the well-known tale, Rumpelstiltskin. Paul Nussbaumer created with

---

[2]James R. Squire, ed. *Response to Literature.* (Champaign, Illinois: National Council of Teachers of English, 1968), p. 3.

From NAIL SOUP by Harve Zemach. Illustrated by Margot Zemach. Copyright © 1964 by Margot Zemach. Reprinted with permission of Follett Publishing Company.

poster paint the colorful pictures that illustrate *Away in a Manger,* a Christmas story told by Mares Nussbaumer. Beautifully illustrated versions of familiar and unfamiliar folktales abound. This is fortunate, for it makes it so much easier and more enjoyable to introduce universal literature to today's children. Folktales are a traditional form of expression. Each tale has been handed down through the ages, and each tale links the young readers of today with a cultural heritage of the past. Many of the folktales portray the dreams of all mankind; many depict the frailties of humanity. Some folktales depict the basic emotions and strengths of people. Some identify the absurdities of life and help children to learn to laugh *at* themselves and to laugh *with* others. Reading and thinking about the themes of folktales will help to develop appreciation for and enjoyment of one's own literary and cultural heritage, as well as the heritage of others. The many picture book versions of these folktales will help, perhaps, to accomplish these goals more quickly and more easily.

Developing Appreciation and Understanding of the Graphic Arts. A child's taste for the beautiful in the visual arts starts as he looks at the illustrations. He should have an opportunity to see a wide variety of art styles and should read many picture books and illustrated books wherein these varieties in styles are employed. Also, it is necessary that he do some close reading, some careful looking at these illustrations.[3] This latter approach to using a picture book is usually taken to mean direct instruction about characteristics of the various styles of art as well as attention to the possible media artists might use to illustrate a story. It means careful appraisal of an illustrated or picture book in terms of specific criteria. The first response one should get from reading literature should be that of enjoyment. Critical reading skills which call for evaluation of the quality of writing used to tell the story, and appraisal of the illustrations that accompany the text may well help the reader to be more discriminating in his reading and will bring more enjoyment to the act of reading itself. Some attention, then, should be given to a book as being one of the graphic arts.

Wide and careful reading of books that are illustrated with beautiful paintings and designs will help the reader to acquire an appreciation for and an understanding of fine art. Careful reading of many books that exemplify quality writing will lead him to be more discriminating in his selection of quality literary selections. There are numerous picture books and other illustrated books that have excellent illustrations in them and that are written well.

Exposure to excellence alone will not develop attitudes of appreciation or discrimination for quality literature or art. Children must be given numerous opportunities to make comparisons with the mediocre as well as with the beautiful selections. They should be asked to compare the work of one book artist with another. They should compare and contrast the ways in which artists have illustrated the same or similar stories. They should compare and contrast the manner in which artists have used the same media; they should be aware of the major characteristics of the various media and of the styles of art available to book artists.

When children write and illustrate their own picture books they learn to appreciate the effort, the talent, and the skills that are neces-

---

[3]Ibid., p. 8.

sary to create a fine book. Children of all ages can engage in this sort of activity. Four-and-five-year-olds, twelve-year-olds, and even adults learn much and find enjoyment in this sort of creative effort.

Four-and-five-year-old kindergarteners in a Milwaukee (Wisconsin) Public School were involved in a "storymaking" project. Throughout the year, the children dictated their stories and then used a variety of media to illustrate them. Their teacher read many excellent picture books to them. They talked about the stories themselves, identifying and evaluating (on the young child's level, of course) plot, setting, characterization, and theme. They talked about the pictures in the books. Whenever the teacher knew what medium an artist had used to make the pictures, she would share this information with the pupils. If she had any biographical information or knew anecdotes about the author or illustrator, this also was shared with the children. By the end of the year, the children had grown in language power (oral expression), in creative thinking ability, and in drawing and painting ability. They were extremely sensitive and alert to various techniques used by book artists; they noticed that the illustrations were done in different styles of art. They were fully cognizant of the individual authors and illustrators of the picture books that were included in their school and library collections.

A sixth grade classroom of children attending a public school in Bloomfield Hills (Michigan) studied carefully the styles of art and the media used by book artists who illustrated the picture books in their school library collection. These pupils were not the least bit hesitant to get picture books from their library. They read the stories—and enjoyed them. Then they studied the aspects of illustrating which have been mentioned here previously. They read articles in *The Horn Book, Elementary English,* and *Publishers' Weekly* that were written about or by book artists. Some of these periodicals were brought in by their teacher, but the children also went to their public library to get the necessary information about the artists they chose to study. Some children, in order to have a more direct source for their information, wrote to artists Ezra Jack Keats, Maurice Sendak, Robert McCloskey, and H. A. Rey. Excitement and delight ran rampant when their letters were answered by these important and talented book artists. Several of the pupils wrote their own stories and tried to illustrate them in the same style, or with the same medium as the artists each had studied. The enthusiasm that this group of sixth graders developed, and the wealth of knowledge for the graphic arts and literature that they acquired, were rewarding to say the least—rewarding for them, and for their teacher, too.

Summary. A reader of any age may be given beautifully illustrated books about almost any subject. He may use these books to help him realize diversified personal or educational objectives. Some of the specific objectives have been discussed in this chapter. Illustrated books can serve as an excellent source from which the reader can derive pleasure, fun, and even laughter. Illustrated books provide a source from which children can view and experience (vicariously) many of the realities of growing up. They can be used to help the young reader form more mature and more adequate concepts of himself and of his ever-expanding world. They can be used to provide the background of experiences and understanding that will help the learner grow in language power. Illustrated books may be used to help the reader acquire a literary and cultural heritage, and they may be used to help the student to understand and appreciate the graphic arts and the fine arts. A few titles of illustrated books that might be used to help children realize these goals have been presented.

SELECTED REFERENCES

ALIKI, (PSEUD. ALIKI BRANDENBERG). *My Five Senses.* New York: Thomas Y. Crowell Company, 1962.
———. *My Hands.* New York: Thomas Y. Crowell Company, 1962.
ANDERSEN, HANS CHRISTIAN. *The Nightingale.* Translated by Eva LeGallienne. Illustrated by Nancy Ekholm Burkert. New York: Harper & Row, Publishers, 1965.
BROWN, MARCIA. *Once a Mouse . . . . . . A Fable Cut in Wood.* New York: Charles Scribner's Sons, 1961.
BROWN, MARGARET WISE. *The Country Noisy Book.* Illustrated by Leonard Weisgard. New York: Harper & Row, Publishers, 1940.
———. *Goodnight Moon.* Illustrated by Clement Hurd. New York: Harper & Row, Publishers, 1947.
BURTON, VIRGINIA LEE. *The Little House.* Boston: Houghton Mifflin Company, 1942.
DALGLIESH, ALICE. *The Bears on Hemlock Mountain.* Illustrated by Helen Sewell. New York: Charles Scribner's Sons, 1952.
ELKIN, BENJAMIN. *The Loudest Noise in the World.* Illustrated by James Daugherty. New York: The Viking Press, Inc., 1954.
EMBERLEY, ED. *Green Says Go.* Boston: Little, Brown & Company, 1968.
FISHER, AILEEN. *In the Middle of the Night.* Illustrated by Adrienne Adams. New York: Thomas Y. Crowell Company, 1965.
FREEMAN, DON. *Dandelion.* New York: Harper & Row, Publishers, 1965.
———. *Mop Top.* New York: The Viking Press, Inc., 1955.
GOUDEY, ALICE E. *Butterfly Time.* Illustrated by Adrienne Adams. New York: Charles Scribner's Sons, 1964.
———. *Houses from the Sea.* Illustrated Adrienne Adams. New York: Charles Scribner's Sons, 1959.

GRIMM, JACOB & WILHELM. *The Shoemaker and the Elves.* Illustrated by
Adrienne Adams. New York: Charles Scribner's Sons, 1960.
HILL, ELIZABETH STARR. *Evan's Corner.* Illustrated by Nancy Grossman. New
York: Holt, Rinehart & Winston, Inc., 1967.
HOBAN, RUSSELL. *A Baby Sister for Frances.* Illustrated by Lillian Hoban. New
York: Harper & Row, Publishers, 1964.
———. *Bedtime for Frances.* Illustrated by Garth Williams. New York: Harper
& Row, Publishers, 1960.
HOLLING, HOLLING C. *Minn of the Mississippi.* Boston: Houghton Mifflin,
1951.
———. *Paddle-to-the-Sea.* Boston: Houghton Mifflin, 1941.
———. *Pagoo.* Boston: Houghton Mifflin, 1957.
———. *Seabird.* Boston: Houghton Mifflin, 1947.
———. *Tree in the Trail.* Boston: Houghton Mifflin, 1942.
ISH-KISHOR, SULAMITH. *The Carpet of Solomon.* Illustrated by Uri Shulevitz.
New York: Pantheon Books, Inc., 1966.
JARRELL, RANDALL. *The Bat Poet.* Illustrated Maurice Sendak. New York: The
Macmillan Company, 1964.
KEATS, EZRA JACK. *John Henry; An American Legend.* New York: Pantheon
Books, Inc., 1965.
———. *Whistle for Willie.* New York: The Viking Press, Inc., 1964.
KRAUSS, RUTH. *The Growing Story.* Illustrated Phyllis Rowand. New York:
Harper & Row, Publishers, 1947.
KUSKIN, KARLA. *Just Like Everyone Else.* New York: Harper & Row, Pub-
lishers, 1959.
LEAR, EDWARD and OGDEN NASH. *The Scroobious Pip.* Illustrated by Nancy
Ekholm Burkert. New York: Harper & Row, Publishers, 1968.
LEXAU, JOAN M. *Every Day a Dragon.* New York: Harper & Row, Publishers,
1967.
———. *Striped Ice Cream.* Philadelphia: J. B. Lippincott Co., 1968.
LIFTON, BETTY JEAN. *The Secret Seller.* New York: W. W. Norton & Company,
Inc., 1968.
McCLOSKEY, ROBERT. *One Morning in Maine.* New York: The Viking Press,
Inc., 1952.
NESS, EVALINE. *Tom Tit Tot.* New York: Charles Scribner's Sons, 1965.
NUSSBAUMER, MARES. *Away in a Manger: A Story of the Nativity.* Illustrated
by Paul Nussbaumer. New York: Harcourt, Brace & World, Inc., 1965.
RANSOME, ARTHUR. *The Fool of the World and the Flying Ship.* Illustrated by
Uri Shulevitz. New York: Farrar, Straus & Giroux, Inc., 1968.
REY, HANS A. *Feed the Animals.* Boston: Houghton Mifflin Company, n.d.
———. *Where's My Baby.* Boston: Houghton Mifflin Company, 1956.
SCHNEIDER, NINA. *While Susie Sleeps.* Illustrated Dagmar Wilson. New York:
William R. Scott, Inc., 1948.
SCHOENHERR, JOHN. *The Barn.* Boston: Atlantic-Little, Brown and Company,
1968.
SENDAK, MAURICE. *Where the Wild Things Are.* New York: Harper & Row,
Publishers, 1963.
SEUSS, DR. (PSEUD. THEODORE S. GEISEL). *And to Think that I Saw It on
Mulberry Street.* New York: Vanguard Press, Inc., 1937.
———. *The Cat in the Hat.* New York: Random House, Inc., 1957.

——. *The 500 Hats of Bartholomew Cubbins.* New York: Vanguard Press, Inc., 1938.

——. *Horton Hatches the Egg.* New York: Random House, Inc., 1940.

——. *The King's Stilts.* New York: Random House, Inc., 1939.

SHOWERS, PAUL. *Follow Your Nose.* Illustrated by Paul Galdone. New York: Thomas Y. Crowell Company, 1963.

——. *Look at Your Eyes.* Illustrated by Paul Galdone. New York: Thomas Y. Crowell Company, 1962.

SLOBODKINA, ESPHYR. *Caps for Sale.* New York: William R. Scott, Inc., 1947.

TUDOR, TASHA, *Linsey Woolsey.* New York: Henry Z. Walck, Inc., 1946.

UDRY, JANICE. *What Mary Jo Shared.* Illustrated by Eleanor Mill. Chicago: Albert Whitman & Company, 1966.

——. *What Mary Jo Wanted.* Illustrated by Eleanor Mill. Chicago: Albert Whitman & Company, 1968.

UNGERER, TOMI. *Moon Man.* New York: Harper & Row, Publishers, 1967.

——. *Zeralda's Ogre.* New York: Harper & Row, Publishers, 1967.

VALENS, EVANS G., JR. *Wildfire.* Illustrated by Clement Hurd. Cleveland: The World Publishing Company, 1963.

WEIK, MARY HAYS. *The Jazz Man.* Illustrated by Ann Grifalconi. New York: Atheneum Publishers, 1966.

WABER, BERNARD. *An Anteater Named Arthur.* Boston: Houghton Mifflin Company, 1967.

WARD, LYND. *The Biggest Bear.* Boston: Houghton Mifflin Company, 1952.

WILDSMITH, BRIAN. *Brian Wildsmith's Birds.* New York: Franklin Watts, Inc., 1967.

——. *Brian Wildsmith's Fishes.* New York: Franklin Watts, Inc., 1968.

——. *Brian Wildsmith's Wild Animals.* New York: Franklin Watts, Inc., 1967.

ZEMACH, HARVE. *Nail Soup.* Illustrated by Margot Zemach. Chicago: Follett Publishing Company, 1964.

——. *Salt.* Illustrated by Margot Zemach. Chicago: Follett Publishing Company, 1965.

——. *The Speckled Hen: a Russian Nursery Rhyme.* Illustrated by Margot Zemach. New York: Holt, Rinehart & Winston, Inc., 1966.

——. *Mommy, Buy Me a China Doll.* Illustrated by Margot Zemach. Chicago: Follett Publishing Company, 1966.

introduction to bibliography
of illustrated children's books

The bibliography that follows constitutes a compilation of books that contain pictures which effectively illustrate the accompanying texts. Some of the books have only a few pictures; others are profusely illustrated. The illustrations in each book are a significant part of the book. Hopefully, each entry serves to exemplify the qualities that were elaborated upon in the chapter entitled "Appraising Illustrations in Children's Books." These qualities are

> something of significance is said;
> audience is understood and respected;
> artistic talent prevails;
> illustrations go beyond the text;
> color (and shading) is used to serve an expressive goal; and
> sizes and shapes of the illustrated books vary.

An attempt was made to include illustrated books that are a representative sampling of the various styles of art as well as of the various media and techniques used by the artists. Illustrated books and picture books for children of from four to sixteen years of age are included in the bibliography.

bibliography of illustrated children's books

ADDAMS, CHARLES. *The Chas. Addams Mother Goose.* Illustrated by Charles Addams. New York: Harper & Row, Publishers, 1967.

Traditional Mother Goose rhymes illustrated in a sophisticated and satirical manner. Ages 9-12.

AIKEN, CONRAD POTTER. *Cats and Bats and Things with Wings.* Illustrated by Milton Glaser. New York: Atheneum Publishers, 1965.

A compilation of sixty witty poems about animals. Illustrations are brilliantly colored paintings done in a unique and expressive style. Ages 5-11.

ANDERSEN, HANS CHRISTIAN. *The Nightingale.* Translated by Eva Le Gallienne. Illustrated by Nancy Ekholm Burkert. New York: Harper & Row, Publishers, 1965.

A familiar Andersen fairy tale illustrated with carefully detailed paintings in a style suggestive of early Chinese screens. Ages 6-10.

———. *Thumbelina.* Illustrated by Adrienne Adams. New York: Charles Scribner's Sons, 1961.

Classic fairy tale illustrated with realistically styled and carefully detailed watercolor paintings. Ages 5-8.

Also Worthy of Note:

ANDERSEN, HANS CHRISTIAN. *The Ugly Duckling.* Illustrated by Adrienne Adams. New York: Charles Scribner's Sons, 1965. Ages 7-10.

ANGLUND, JOAN WALSH. *In a Pumpkin Shell.* Illustrated by Joan Walsh Anglund. New York: Harcourt, Brace & World, Inc., 1960.

A nursery rhyme and alphabet book illustrated with colored and pen-and-ink drawings. Ages 3-7.

———. *Nibble, Nibble Mousekin.* Illustrated by Joan Walsh Anglund. New York: Harcourt, Brace & World, Inc., 1962.

A picture book and simplified version of Grimms' *Hansel and Gretel.* Illustrations are in the detailed and ingenuous style typical of Anglund's work. They are done in full color and line technique. Ages 5-8.

ARDIZZONE, EDWARD and AINGELDA. *The Little Girl and the Tiny Doll.* Illustrated by Edward Ardizzone. New York: The Delacorte Press, 1967.

A miniature doll, cold and frightened because she was abandoned in the self-service freezer in a grocery store, is found by a little girl who brings it warm handmade clothing and eventually assumes ownership of the doll. Illustrations are line and wash drawings, alternating in mustard and lavender colors. Ages 4-7.

BALET, JAN B. *The Gift; A Portuguese Christmas Tale.* Illustrated by Jan B. Balet. New York: The Delacorte Press, 1967.

Joanjo gives the Christ Child his appreciation of a sunbeam, a moonbeam, and the twinkle of the evening star, whereas others bring lovely gifts of flowers, food, and music. Illustrations are doll-like figures dressed in traditional peasant costumes, all of which are gaily colored. Ages 4-6.

———. *Joanjo, A Portuguese Tale.* Illustrated by Jan B. Balet. New York: The Delacorte Press, 1967.

Joanjo, a small boy in a Portuguese fishing village dreams he travels and becomes rich and important and greedy, then awakens convinced that a fisherman's life is for him. Illustrations are in full color and reflect the spirit of the tale. Ages 5-8.

BEATTY, JEROME, JR. *Bob Fulton's Amazing Soda-Pop Stretcher.* Illustrated by Gahan Wilson. New York: William R. Scott, Inc., Publisher, 1963.

A parody on the politics and the scientific advances of the Space Age, this is a story about the events that occurred after a boy accidently invents a non-friction producing gook. Illustrated with clever cartoon-style sketches. Ages 9-14.

BEMELMANS, LUDWIG. *Madeline.* Illustrated by Ludwig Bemelmans. New York: The Viking Press, Inc., 1939.

A humorous account in rhymed couplets which tells what happens when Madeline, one of twelve girls attending a French boarding school in Paris, is taken to a hospital for an appendectomy. Illustrations are in the expressionistic style and are colored. Ages 5-8.

BISHOP, ELIZABETH. *The Ballad of the Burglar of Babylon.* Illustrated by Ann Grifalconi. New York: Farrar, Straus, & Giroux, Inc., 1968.

Micucu, an escaped convict and murderer, no longer treated as human by society, is chased through the hills like a dangerous animal and finally killed. Exquisitely styled woodcuts emphasize the message of this ballad—Micucu's death on Babylon is "an immortal archetypal myth of the scapegoat." Ages 12-16.

BONSALL, CROSBY. *I'll Show You Cats.* Illustrated by Ylla (pseud. Koffler Camilla). New York: Harper & Row, Publishers, 1964.

A compilation of action-filled photographs of cats and kittens, accompanied by a brief but imaginative text. Ages 4-8.

BONTEMPS, ARNA. *Lonesome Boy.* Illustrated by Feliks Topolski. Boston: Houghton Mifflin Company, 1955.

A symbolic account of events involving Bubber, a New Orleans boy who loved his trumpet, and falls under the spell of jazz. Exquisite expressionistic line drawings interpret this mood story. Ages 12 and up.

BORACK, BARBARA. *Grandpa.* Illustrated by Ben Shecter. New York: Harper & Row, Publishers, 1967.

A little girl guilelessly tells about the fun she has with her grandfather. Illustrated with simple drawings done in color. Ages. 4-7.

BRANDENBERG, ALIKI. *Three Gold Pieces; A Greek Folktale.* Illustrated by Aliki. New York: Pantheon Books, Inc., 1967.

A peasant who worked far from home for ten years, exchanges his total earnings of three pieces of gold for three pieces of advice, avoids death twice, and returns home with pockets and a bundle filled with gold. Illustrations consist of full-color paintings alternating with black and white drawings. Ages 5-8.

BRENNER, ANITA. *The Timid Ghost; or What Would You Do with A Sackful of Gold?* Illustrated by Jean Charlot. New York: William R. Scott, Inc., 1966.

A retelling of a Mexican folktale about a ghost who wanders around seeking a right answer to his question, "What would you do with a sackful of gold?" Three-color line drawings illustrate this ironic tale. Ages 9-12.

BRENNER, BARBARA. *Mr. Tall and Mr. Small.* Illustrated by Tomi Ungerer. New York: William R. Scott, Inc., 1966.

A giraffe and a mouse are almost trapped by a forest fire as they argue about which one is the better size. They realize that each size has its unique advantages as they find their way to safety by combining what the mouse hears when he puts his ear to the ground and what the giraffe sees when he looks over the treetops. Humorous cartoon-type drawings in four colors illustrate the story. Ages 4-7.

BROWN, MARCIA. *Backbone of the King; The Story of Paka'a and His Son Ku.* Illustrated by Marcia Brown. New York: Charles Scribner's Sons, 1966.

A retelling of a Hawaiian legend concerning the events that brought about the exiled Paka'a's restoration to his rightful place as personal attendant, or "backbone of the king." The author has used authentic Hawaiian names and chants to portray effectively the ancient Hawaiian culture. Exquisite linoleum block prints illustrate this legend. Ages 10-14.

———. *Cinderella.* Illustrated by Marcia Brown. New York: Charles Scribner's Sons, 1954.

A picture book version of a favorite fairy tale, illustrated with delicate drawings in pen line and colored crayon in a style suggestive of period French art. Ages 5-8.

———. *Stone Soup.* Illustrated by Marcia Brown. New York: Charles Scribner's Sons, 1947.

An old falktale which tells how the soldiers tricked the villagers into providing them with all of the ingredients for a soup "fit for a king." Illustrated with humorous red and black drawings in a style suggestive of peasant art. Ages 6-9.

———. *Once a Mouse . . . A Fable Cut in Wood.* Illustrated by Marcia Brown. New York: Charles Scribner's Sons, 1961.

An Indian fable about a mouse that is changed into a cat, then a dog, and a tiger, and back again into a timid mouse. Illustrated with colored woodcut prints. Ages 5-9.

98   BIBLIOGRAPHY OF ILLUSTRATED CHILDREN'S BOOKS

BROWN, MARGARET WISE. *The Dead Bird.* Illustrated by Remy Charlip. New
York: William R. Scott, Inc., 1958.
Children find a dead bird, conduct a funeral service for it, and soon
forget about it as they play. Firm and clear expressionistic paintings
illustrate this brief and simple story. Ages 4-6.
BROWNSTONE, CECILY. *All Kinds of Mothers.* Illustrated by Miriam Brofsky.
New York: David McKay Co., Inc., 1969.
An imaginative picture book which stresses that mothers may differ in
some respects but that they are all alike in that each one has "pitchers
of love" for her child. Illustrated with black and red cartoon-styled drawings. Ages 4-9.
BRYANT, SARA CONE. *The Burning Rice Fields.* Illustrated by Mamoru Funai.
New York: Holt, Rinehart & Winston, Inc., 1963.
A brief and simplified version of the Japanese folktale about a man who
burned the rice fields on top of a mountain to save the lives of the villagers who were threatened by a tidal wave. Illustrated with double
spread pictures done with pastels. Ages 5-8.
BRYSON, BERNARDA. *Gilgamesh.* Illustrated by Bernarda Bryson. New York:
Holt, Rinehart & Winston, Inc., 1967.
A retelling of a myth about the Sumerian god-king Gilgamesh. Stunning
watercolor paintings and pastel drawings illustrate this large picture
book. Ages 10-14.
BURCH, ROBERT. *Joey's Cat.* Illustrated by Don Freeman. New York: The Vik-
ing Press, Inc., 1969.
Joey's cat has kittens but almost loses them to a possum. Illustrations are
blue and black sketches done in a free representational style. Ages 5-8.
BURNS, ROBERT. *Hand in Hand We'll Go; Ten Poems.* Illustrated by Nonny
Hogrogian. New York: Thomas Y. Crowell Company, 1965.
An inviting compilation of ten poems composed by the Scottish poet,
Robert Burns. Illustrated with colored woodcuts which aptly evoke moods
and scenes of the poems. Included is a glossary of the Scottish words.
Ages 12 and up.
BURTON, VIRGINIA LEE. *The Little House.* Illustrated by Virginia Lee Burton.
Boston: Houghton Mifflin Company, 1942.
A picture book account of a little house in the country that gradually
finds itself surrounded by skyscrapers and the busy traffic and human
activities typical of a city. Illustrated with appropriate realistic and
detailed watercolor paintings. Ages 5-8.
CARIGIET, ALOIS. *Anton the Goatherd.* Illustrated by Alois Carigiet. New York:
Henry Z. Walck, Inc., 1966.
A young Alpine goatherd searches for three runaway goats. Distinctive
and colorful illustrations portray the Swiss village and the meadow in
which this story is set. Ages 6-10.
CARLE, ERIC. *1, 2, 3 to the Zoo.* Illustrated by Eric Carle. Cleveland: The
World Publishing Company, 1968.
An imaginative number book without text. Illustrations consist of double-
page spreads, each of which contains a number and a corresponding number of zoo animals in a train car. A little mouse travels along throughout,
chatting with each "set" of animals. Illustrations are done in the collage
and poster paint technique. Ages 2-7.

CARROLL, RUTH and LATROBE. *Tough Enough*. Illustrated by Ruth Carroll. New York: Oxford University Press, Inc., 1954.

An exciting story set in the Great Smoky Mountains of North Carolina; deals with mischievous puppy who is thought to have killed chickens, is exonerated and becomes a hero when he saves the children from a flash flood. Illustrated with realistic action-filled pencil drawings. Ages 7-10.

CAUDILLE, REBECCA. *Did You Carry the Flag Today, Charley?* Illustrated by Nancy Grossman. New York: Holt, Rinehart & Winston, Inc., 1966.

Charley, an independent and curious five-year-old, meets with some exciting circumstances during a summer school for four and five-year-olds in the Appalachian Mountain area. Appropriate line drawings highlight his experiences. Ages 5-8.

CHONZ, SELINA. *A Bell for Ursli*. Illustrated by Alois Carigiet. New York: Henry Z. Walck, Inc., 1953.

Ursli finds a bell to use during the festival celebrating the arrival of spring. Exquisite colorful paintings depicting Swiss mountain villages add much to this story. Ages 5-8.

Also Worthy of Note:

CHONZ, SELINA. *Florina and the Wild Bird*. Illustrated by Alois Carigiet. New York: Henry Z. Walck, Inc., 1967. Ages 5-8.

CHONZ, SELINA. *The Snowstorm*. Illustrated by Alois Carigiet. New York: Henry Z. Walck, Inc., 1958. Ages 5-8.

COATSWORTH, ELIZABETH JANE. *Troll Weather*. Illustrated by Ursula Arndt. New York: The Macmillan Company, 1967.

Selma gathers information about trolls and learns that different people have different ideas about them. Black and white drawings highlight sprightly moods of the tale and the various aspects of life in the Norwegian mountains. Ages 7-10.

COLE, WILLIAM, ed. *Oh, What Nonsense*. Illustrated by Tomi Ungerer. New York: The Viking Press, Inc., 1966.

An anthology of fifty nonsense verses composed by well-known poets, Laura E. Richards, John Ciardi, David McCord, and Spike Milligan. Black and white drawings very effectively reflect the gaiety and the nonsensical spirit of the poems. Ages 6-11.

COONEY, BARBARA. *Chanticleer and the Fox*. Illustrated by Barbara Cooney. New York: Thomas Y. Crowell Company, 1958.

An adaptation of one of *The Canterbury Tales*, this fable emphasizes the dangers of accepting flattery. Illustrated in a style reminiscent of illuminated manuscripts and includes numerous detailed scenes and settings typical of the England of Chaucer's time. Ages 7-10.

DAHL, ROALD. *Charlie and the Chocolate Factory*. Illustrated by Joseph Schindelman. New York: Alfred A. Knopf, Inc., 1964.

A humorous and fanciful account of the experiences had by the five children who find gold seals on their chocolate bars thus enabling them to tour the mysterious, locked chocolate factory. Clever cartoon-styled pen sketches illustrate this creative story. Ages 9-13.

DALGLIESH, ALICE. *The Bears on Hemlock Mountain.* Illustrated by Helen Sewell. New York: Charles Scribner's Sons, 1952.

A tension-filled story telling what happens to Jonathan when he meets two bears on Hemlock Mountain while returning with a big kettle that he had borrowed from his aunt. Ages 5-9.

DAUGHERTY, JAMES. *Daniel Boone.* Illustrated by James Daugherty. New York: The Viking Press, Inc., 1939.

A narrative biography in which Daniel Boone is zestfully portrayed as a hero, and aspects of his exploits and personality are depicted accurately within the setting of America's westward expansion. Illustrations are bold and realistic line drawings in brown, green, and black. Ages 10-14.

D'AULAIRE, EDGAR and INGRI. *Abraham Lincoln.* Illustrated by Edgar and Ingri D'Aulaire. Garden City, N.Y.: Doubleday & Company, Inc., 1939, 1957.

A brief biography of Lincoln presented in picture book format. Illustrations for first edition were large stone lithograph prints in full-color alternating with large black and white drawings; those for the revised edition were made with acetates. Ages 8-12.

DE LA MARE, WALTER. *Jack and the Beanstalk.* Illustrated by Joseph Low. New York: Alfred A. Knopf, Inc., 1959.

A picture book (long and thin in shape) version of the well-known tale. Illustrated with bold and heavy, but whimsical, line drawings. Ages 4-9.

DEREGNIERS, BEATRICE SCHENK. *The Arbraham Lincoln Joke Book.* Illustrated by William Lehey Cummings. New York: Random House, Inc., 1965.

A compilation of jokes and humorous anecdotes told by or about Abraham Lincoln. Lively cartoon-style drawings match the mood of the jokes and anecdotes.

———. *May I Bring a Friend?* Illustrated by Beni Montresor. New York: Atheneum Publishers, 1964.

A childlike and humorous story of a small boy who brings his friends (giraffe, hippopotamus, and lions) with him when the King and Queen invite him to tea, dinner, lunch, breakfast, Halloween, and Apple Pie Day. Illustrations, which resemble stage settings, are basic line drawings in three colors. Ages 5-8.

Also Worthy of Note:

MONTRESOR, BENI. *The Witches of Venice.* Illustrated by Beni Montresor. New York: Alfred A. Knopf, Inc., 1963.

DICKENS, CHARLES. *A Christmas Carol in Prose; Being a Ghost Story of Christmas.* Illustrated by Philip Reed. New York: Atheneum Publishers, 1966.

Numerous colored woodcuts aptly convey the mood and events of this familiar story. Ages 12-16.

DUNN, JUDY. *Things.* Photographs by Phoebe and Tris Dunn. Garden City, N.Y.: Doubleday & Company, Inc., 1968.

Colored photographs effectively illustrate a variety of "things" children can do, hold, taste, and wonder about. Text is brief and appropriate. Ages 4-10.

From THINGS by Judy Dunn. Illustrated by Phoebe and Tris Dunn. Copyright © 1968 by Doubleday & Company, Inc. Reprinted with permission of the publisher.

DUNNING, STEPHEN; LUEDERS, EDWARD; and SMITH, HUGH. *Reflections on a Gift of Watermelon Pickle and Other Modern Verse*. Illustrated with photographs. Glenview, Ill.: Scott, Foresman & Company, 1966.

A compilation of 114 selections of modern verse, illustrated with striking photographs that complement, interpret, or extend the poems. Ages 12 and up.

EINSEL, WALTER. *Did You Ever See?* Illustrated by Walter Einsel. New York: William R. Scott, Inc., 1962.

A compilation of imaginative and humorous rhymes. Illustrations are heavy line drawings in bold bright colors. Ages 4-6.

ELKIN, BENJAMIN. *Why the Sun Was Late*. Illustrated by Jerome Snyder. New York: Parents' Magazine Press, 1966.

A cumulative African folktale about the series of events that occurred when a small fly alighted on a leaf of an old weak tree in the jungle causing the tree to crash. Illustrated with appropriate double-spread colored pictures. Ages 4-8.

EMBERLEY, BARBARA. *Drummer Hoff*. Illustrated by Ed Emberley. Englewood Cliffs, N.J.: Prentice-Hall, Inc., 1967.

An adaptation in cumulative pattern of a folk verse about the building of a cannon. Illustrations are stylized woodcuts in gay, brilliant shades and are filled with humorous details. Caldecott Medal award winner, 1968. Ages 4-8.

———. *One Wide River to Cross*. Illustrated by Ed Emberley. Englewood Cliffs, N.J.: Prentice-Hall, Inc., 1966.

A counting book which interprets the folk song about groups of animals moving into Noah's ark. Illustrated with precise black woodcuts on brilliantly colored pages. Words and music for the song are included. Ages 5-8.

Also Worthy of Note:

EMBERLEY, BARBARA. *The Story of Paul Bunyan.* Illustrated by Ed Emberley. Englewood Cliffs, N.J.: Prentice-Hall, Inc., 1963. Ages 8-12.

EMBERLEY, ED. *Green Says Go.* Illustrated by Ed Emberley. Boston: Little, Brown and Company, 1968.

ENRIGHT, ELIZABETH. *Tatsinda.* Illustrated by Irene Haas. New York: Harcourt, Brace & World, Inc., 1963.

Written in the style of a traditional fairy tale, this is an original story that is exciting and romantic and that emphasizes the senselessness of conformity. The illustrations match the mood and action of this charming story and are done with pencil, ink, and watercolor in full color. Ages 9-12.

Also Worthy of Note:

ENRIGHT, ELIZABETH. *Zeee.* Illustrated by Irene Haas. New York: Harcourt, Brace & World, Inc., 1965. Ages 7-10.

ESTES, ELEANOR. *Miranda the Great.* Illustrated by Edward Ardizzone. New York: Harcourt, Brace & World, Inc., 1967.

A humorous account of what happened to the cat, Miranda, her daughter, and the thirty-three cats they rescued as they fled Rome to avoid the barbarians and made their way to the Colosseum ruins. Illustrated with line drawings that express the pathos and humor of this narrative. Ages 9-12.

ETS, MARIE HALL. *Gilberto and the Wind.* Illustrated by Marie Hall Ets. New York: The Viking Press, Inc., 1965.

A simple childlike account of the many ways a small boy can "play" with the wind. The drawings are done in black and white (except for the brown-skinned Mexican boy), and they are printed on gray paper. They depict the details and moods of the text very well. Ages 3-5.

E-YEH-SHURE. *I Am a Pueblo Indian Girl.* Illustrated by Quincy Tahoma, Tony Martinez, Alan Houser, and Gerald Nailor. New York: William Morrow & Co., Inc., 1939.

An interpretation of the daily life activities of a Pueblo Indian girl, including details about her home, her clothes, corn planting, hairwashing, and making bread. Illustrations were done by four Indian artists and include eleven striking watercolors. Ages 10-14.

FENNER, CAROL. *Christmas Tree on the Mountain.* Illustrated by Carol Fenner. New York: Harcourt, Brace & World, Inc., 1966.

Three children climb up snow-covered mountain slopes searching for a perfect Christmas tree. Pastel drawings provoke a joyous response to the sights and the feel of winter. Ages 5-8.

FISHER, AILEEN L. *My Mother and I.* Illustrated by Kazue Mizumura. New York: Thomas Y. Crowell Company, 1967.

A little girl observes and thinks about the many creatures in nature that have no mothers and learns to appreciate her own mother more. Illustrated with watercolors. Ages 5-8.

FLORA, JAMES. *The Day the Cow Sneezed.* Illustrated by James Flora. New York: Harcourt, Brace & World, Inc., 1957.

A cumulative tale-type story of what happens when a cow sneezes. The illustrations, done in gouache, are action-packed and match the hilarious chain reaction that occurs when the cow sneezes. Ages 4-8.

FRANCOISE, (pseud. FRANCOISE SEIGNOBOSC). *Jeanne Marie Counts Her Sheep.* New York: Charles Scribner's Sons, 1951.

A counting book cleverly concocted—Jeanne Marie dreams of the many lambs her pet sheep will have and what she could buy from their sale. Drawings are refreshingly childlike and are in bright, opaque colors. Ages 3-6.

FRASCONI, ANTONIO. *See and Say.* Illustrated by Antonio Frasconi. New York: Harcourt, Brace & World, Inc., 1955.

A picture book in which many different familiar objects are pictured, with the name of each given and phonetically pronounced in four languages—English, Italian, French, and Spanish. Illustrations are printed in strong colors and are strikingly simple woodcut prints. Ages 6-9.

———. *The Snow and the Sun.* Illustrated by Antonio Frasconi. New York: Harcourt, Brace & World, Inc., 1961.

A south American cumulative rhyme presented in English and Spanish. Illustrated with woodcuts in bold opaque colors and in black and white. Ages 6-10.

Also Worthy of Note:

FRASCONI, ANTONIO. *See Again, Say Again.* Illustrated by Antonio Frasconi. New York: Harcourt, Brace & World, Inc., 1964. Ages 7-9.

FREEMAN, DON. *Dandelion.* Illustrated by Don Freeman. New York: The Viking Press, Inc., 1964.

A vain but lovable lion is not recognized by the hostess when he arrives at a party too dressed up. Amusing drawings convey the humor of this entertaining picture book story. Ages 4-8.

GÁG, WANDA. *Millions of Cats.* Illustrated by Wanda Gág. New York: Coward-McCann, Inc., 1928.

An imaginative folktale-type story about a lonely little old man and a little old lady who acquire a cat that changes from a scrawny little cat to a creature of beauty. Illustrated with black and white illustrations that match perfectly the simple, direct, and repetitious text. Ages 4-6.

Also Worthy of Note:

GÁG, WANDA. *Nothing at All.* Illustrated by Wanda Gág. New York: Coward-McCann, Inc., 1941. Ages 3-7.

GARTHWAITE, MARION. *The Twelfth Night Santons.* Illustrated by Winifred Lubell. Garden City, N.Y.: Doubleday & Company, Inc., 1965.

An account of Pierre, a young and reluctant sheepherder from Provence, who is led by a wandering sheep to a clay bed where the boy molds his first santon, a small nativity scene figure. Illustrations are colorful, and aptly portray the village and its famous santons. Ages 7-11.

104   BIBLIOGRAPHY OF ILLUSTRATED CHILDREN'S BOOKS

GLUBOK, SHIRLEY. *The Art of Ancient Mexico.* Photographs by Alfred H. Tamarin. New York: Harper & Row, Publishers, 1968.

A description of artifacts that typify the art and culture of the civilizations of ancient Mexico. Photographs of the art objects are clearly reproduced. Ages 9-14. (Representative of an art series).

———. *Discovering Tut-Ankh-Amen's Tomb.* Foreword by Eric Young. New York: The Macmillan Company, 1968.

Methods of excavation, the preservation of fragile objects, the Egyptian burial customs are discussed in this abridgment and adaptation of *The Tomb of Tut-ankh-amen* by Howard Carter and A. C. Mace. Copiously illustrated with reproductions of photographs taken at the time of the excavation. Ages 11-16.

GOUDEY, ALICE E. *Houses from the Sea.* Illustrated by Adrienne Adams. New York: Charles Scribner's Sons, 1959.

A quick guide for identification of common seashells. Watercolor paintings that illustrate this picture book are representational, detailed, and exact. Ages 5-9.

GRAMATKY, HARDIE. *Little Toot.* Illustrated by Hardie Gramatky. New York: G. P. Putnam's Sons, 1939.

An account of a lazy, irresponsible tugboat that reforms and makes a heroic rescue. Illustrations are cartoon-style, done in watercolor, and match this hilarious personified tale. Ages 5-8.

Also Worthy of Note:

GRAMATKY, HARDIE. *Bolivar.* Illustrated by Hardie Gramatky. New York: G. P. Putnam's Sons, 1961. Ages 5-8.

GREENFELD, HOWARD. *Marc Chagall.* Illustrated with reproductions. Chicago: Follett Publishing Company, 1967.

A personal biography of the contemporary Russian-born painter. Illustrated with sixteen full-color reproductions of the artist's work plus some black and white prints. Ages 11-15.

GRIFALCONI, ANN. *City Rhythms.* Illustrated by Ann Grifalconi. Indianapolis: The Bobbs-Merrill Co., Inc., 1966.

An alert, small Negro boy notices the sights and sounds of the city and re-creates the rhythm of these activities by drumming out the beat on instruments made from buckets, glasses, and sticks. Illustrated with dramatic, colored drawings. Ages 5-8.

GRIMM BROTHERS. *The Four Clever Brothers.* Illustrated by Felix Hoffmann. New York: Harcourt, Brace & World, Inc., 1967.

The traditional tale of four brothers each of whom becomes a master of his chosen trade. Illustrations are clear-cut and rich-colored line drawings that reflect the wit and vitality of the tale. Ages 4-8.

———. *The Good-for-Nothings.* Illustrated by Hans Fischer. New York: Harcourt, Brace & World, Inc., 1957.

A picture book version of the adventures of Chanticleer, the rooster, and his wife as they are homeward bound in a nutshell carriage drawn by a goose. Detailed pen-and-ink sketches highlight this sprightly and humorous folktale. Ages 4-8.

————. *Snow White and Rose Red.* Illustrated by Barbara Cooney. New York: The Delacorte Press, 1966.

Spirited full-color drawings convey the charm of this simple adaptation of the familiar fanciful tale. Ages 5-10.

————. *The Twelve Dancing Princesses.* Illustrated by Uri Shulevitz. New York: Charles Scribner's Sons, 1966.

A facsimile of the first German edition of the now familiar Munster tale. Two-dimensional sketches in bright colors convey the spirit of this folktale. Ages 5-10.

Also Worthy of Note:

GRIMM BROTHERS. *The Shoemaker and the Elves.* Illustrated by Adrienne Adams. New York: Charles Scribner's Sons, 1960. Ages 5-8.

————. *The Traveling Musicians.* Illustrated by Hans Fischer, New York: Harcourt, Brace & World, Inc., 1955. Ages 4-8.

HAMILTON, VIRGINIA. *Zeely.* Illustrated by Symeon Shimin. New York: The Macmillan Company, 1967.

An imaginative eleven-year-old Negro girl eventually learns to differentiate between her daydreams and reality. The illustrations for this fine study of character and of personal relationships are particularly effective. Ages 10-13.

HARRIS, CHRISTIE. *Raven's Cry.* Illustrated by Bill Reid. New York: Atheneum Publishers, 1966.

A narrative description of Haida customs and beliefs during the reign of the last three great Stastas Eagle chiefs, and the effects of the North American Indian's contact with the white man's civilization. Although relatively few in number, the black and white line drawings masterfully illustrate the account. They are done in authentic Haida style. Ages 12-16.

HAUGAARD, ERIK CHRISTIAN. *Hakon of Rogen's Saga.* Illustrated by Leo and Diane Dillon. Boston: Houghton Mifflin Company, 1963.

A descriptive and gripping first person narrative that tells how thirteen-year-old Hakon of Rogen regained his birthright to become ruler of the rocky island of Rogen, in Norway, at the end of the Viking period. Illustrations are intricate woodcuts in black and white. Ages 11-15.

Also Worthy of Note:

HAUGAARD, ERIK CHRISTIAN. *A Slave's Tale.* Illustrated by Leo and Diane Dillon. Boston: Houghton Mifflin Company, 1965. Ages 11-15.

HILL, ELIZABETH STARR. *Evan's Corner.* Illustrated by Nancy Grossman. New York: Holt, Rinehart & Winston, Inc., 1967.

Evan, a member of a family of eight children, provides peace of his own— a corner in a two-room apartment, but finds he is happy only when helping his brother fix up his corner. Illustrations add to the feelings of warmth and sensitivity that prevail throughout this story. Ages 5-8.

HOBAN, RUSSELL. *Bedtime for Frances.* Illustrated by Garth Williams. New York: Harper & Row, Publishers, 1960.

Frances, a little badger, finds many excuses for not going to sleep. Illustrations are carefully detailed, realistically styled black and white sketches. Ages 4-7.

HODGES, MARGARET. *The Wave.* Illustrated by Blair Lent. Boston: Houghton Mifflin Company, 1964.

A picture book version of the Japanese folktale about an old man who sets fire to his rice fields on the mountain in order to save the villagers from a tidal wave. Illustrations are effective cardboard cutout prints in watercolor. Ages 9-12.

Also Worthy of Note:

SMALL, ERNEST. *Baba Yaga.* Illustrated by Blair Lent. Boston: Houghton Mifflin Company, 1966. Ages 6-10.

HOFFMANN, FELIX. *A Boy Went Out to Gather Pears.* Illustrated by Felix Hoffmann. New York: Harcourt, Brace & World, Inc., 1966.

A traditional, gay cumulative verse that tells about a boy who was sent out to gather pears. Illustrated with amusing prints in full color. Ages 4-7.

Also Worthy of Note:

HOFFMANN, FELIX. *Rapunzel.* Illustrated by Felix Hoffmann. New York: Harcourt, Brace & World, Inc., 1961. Ages 6-9.

HOGE, DOROTHY. *The Black Heart of Indri.* Illustrated by Janina Domanska. New York: Charles Scribner's Sons, 1966.

A retelling of the Chinese version of a fantasy about an ugly, frog-shaped creature who changes into a handsome prince through the love of a headman's daughter. Large illustrations done in a style suggestive of Chinese folk art portray the mood and setting of this nineteenth century folktale. Ages 4-10.

HOLL, ADELAIDE. *The Rain Puddle.* Illustrated by Roger Duvoisin. New York: Lothrop, Lee & Shepard Co., Inc., 1965.

A simple folktale describing a little hen and others when they see their reflection in a rain puddle. Illustrated with clear-cut, brightly colored drawings. Ages 3-6.

HOLLING, HOLLING C. *Paddle-to-the-Sea.* Illustrated by Holling C. Holling. Boston: Houghton Mifflin Company, 1941.

A hand-carved boat travels over the Great Lakes and Niagara Falls to the coast of Newfoundland. Large representational paintings in full-color and black and white sketches illustrate this episodic story. Ages 9-12.

HURLIMANN, BETTINA. *Barry; the Story of a Brave St. Bernard.* Illustrated by Paul Nussbaumer. New York: Harcourt, Brace & World, Inc., 1968.

A picture book presentation of Barry, the St. Bernard dog that won fame for its rescue work with the monks of the great St. Bernard hospice in the Swiss Alps at the time of Napoleon. Illustrations are black and white marginal drawings and full-page paintings which depict mood, scene, and action. Ages 5-10.

———. *William Tell and His Son.* Translated by Elizabeth D. Crawford. Illustrated by Paul Nussbaumer. New York: Harcourt, Brace & World, Inc., 1967.

A shortened picture book version of Tell, the famous Swiss legendary hero. Illustrated with full-color poster paintings and line drawings.

IRVING, WASHINGTON. *Rip Van Winkle.* Illustrations by Arthur Rackham. Philadelphia: J. B. Lippincott Co., 1967.

A familiar narrative illustrated effectively with full-color drawings and several black and white drawings. Ages 11-14.

JARRELL, RANDALL. *The Bat Poet.* Illustrated by Maurice Sendak. New York: The Macmillan Company, 1964.

A little brown bat, unable to sleep during the day, notices for the first time details about the owl, the mockingbird, and the chipmunk. He makes poems about them as well as his own bat babyhood. Illustrations are black and white fine pen-and-ink drawings that look like steel engravings.

JOHNSON, CROCKETT. (pseud. David Johnson Leisk). *Harold and the Purple Crayon.* Illustrated by Crockett Johnson. New York: Harper & Row, Publishers, 1957.

The simple and humorous fantasy of a small boy who draws himself in and out of adventures with a purple crayon. Illustrated with diagramatic, cartoon-style sketches. Ages 3-6.

KAY, HELEN. *Man and Mastiff; The Story of the St. Bernard Dog through History,* New York: The Macmillan Company, 1967.

A treatise describing the domestication and the characteristics of the St. Bernard dog and the role it played in the Switzerland mountain snow rescue work by the monks of St. Bernard's hospice. The author's used historical, legendary, and scientific sources as references. Illustrations are photographs and old prints. Ages 10-14.

KEATS, EZRA JACK. *Peter's Chair.* Illustrated by Ezra Jack Keats. New York: Harper & Row, Publishers, 1967.

Peter is upset when his new little sister is given his crib and his high chair. He decides to run away and plans to take his dog and his little blue chair with him. He changes his mind when he discovers that he has grown too big for the chair and suggests that it be painted pink for his sister. Illustrations done in collage in bright colors. Ages 4-8.

Also Worthy of Note:

KEATS, EZRA JACK. *John Henry; An American Legend.* Illustrated by Ezra Jack Keats. New York: Pantheon Books, Inc., 1965. Ages 6-10.

KEATS, EZRA JACK. *The Snowy Day.* Illustrated by Ezra Jack Keats. New York: The Viking Press, Inc., 1962. Ages 4-8.

KEATS, EZRA JACK. *Whistle for Willie.* Illustrated by Ezra Jack Keats. New York: The Viking Press, Inc., 1964. Ages 4-8.

Illustration for PETER'S CHAIR, written and illustrated by Ezra Jack Keats. Copyright © 1967 by Ezra Jack Keats. Reprinted with permission of Harper & Row, Publishers.

KINGMAN, LEE. *Peter's Long Walk*. Illustrated by Barbara Cooney. Garden City, N.Y.: Doubleday & Company, Inc., 1953.

Told that, when he is five years old, he will be able to go to school and will find playmates there, lonely Peter walks to the village the morning after his fifth birthday. The illustrations capture the spirit of the story told in rhyme, and they comply with the content. Ages 4-7.

KRASILOVSKY, PHYLLIS. *The Cow Who Fell in the Canal*. Illustrated by Peter Spier. Garden City, N.Y.: Doubleday & Company, Inc., 1957.

Hendrika, a Dutch cow, falls into the canal, climbs onto a raft, and floats down to the city. Detailed illustrations are in gay colors; many of them are double-page spreads. All of them afford a view of Holland's country-side and city streets and record Hendrika's sight-seeing cruise down the canal. Ages 4-7.

KRAUSS, RUTH. *The Growing Story.* Illustrated by Phyllis Rowand. New York: Harper & Row, Publishers, 1947.

A little boy watches the many animals and plants around him grow but doesn't realize that he has grown, too, until late autumn when he brings out his last year's warm clothes. Simple illustrations in bright colors. Ages 4-6.

KUSKIN, KARLA. *In the Flaky Frosty Morning.* Illustrated by Karla Kuskin. New York: Harper & Row, Publishers, 1969.

A snowman tells in verse how he got his arms and legs, hat and nose, only to loose them. Illustrated with quaint drawings that match the freshness and sparkle of a winter day. Ages 4-7.

————. *Just Like Everyone Else.* Illustrated by Karla Kuskin. New York: Harper & Row, Publishers, 1959.

A little boy gets up in the morning to go through the regular routine tasks of getting dressed, having breakfast, saying goodbye to his family and dog, and then flies off to school. Charming detailed sketches illustrate this humorous story. Ages 3-6.

LANG, ANDREW. *The Twelve Dancing Princesses.* Illustrated by Adrienne Adams. New York: Holt, Rinehart & Winston, Inc., 1966.

An extended romantic version of the famous fairy tale, drawn from French sources. Vividly-colored illustrations convey the gay spirit and are suggestive of Gallic art. Ages 5-10.

LANGSTAFF, JOHN. *Frog Went A-Courtin'.* Illustrated by Feodor Rojankovsky. New York: Harcourt, Brace & World, Inc., 1955.

A picture book version of the old ballad about the frog and the mouse. Illustrations done in crayon, brush, and ink, are gay and colorful. The music for the ballad, which is sung in the southern Appalachian Mountain area, is included. Ages 5-7.

LAWRENCE, JACOB. *Harriet and the Promised Land.* Illustrated by Jacob Lawrence. New York: Simon and Schuster, Inc., 1968.

A story in verse about Harriet Tubman, Negro slave who was active in the Underground Railroad Movement. Illustrated with large full-color expressionistic paintings (poster paint). Ages 9-14.

LEAR, EDWARD, and NASH, OGDEN. *The Scroobious Pip.* Illustrated by Nancy Ekholm Burkert. New York: Harper & Row, Publishers, 1968.

Rhythmic nonsense verse which tells how all the animals in the world gathered around a strange creature. Quiet, subtle colors are used in representational brush and ink drawings that are detailed and exact. Ages 8-12.

LEEKLEY, THOMAS B. *The World of Manabozho; Tales of the Chippewa Indians.* Illustrations by Yeffe Kimball. New York: Vanguard Press, Inc., 1965.

A compilation of tales and episodic accounts about Manabozho, a legendary hero of the Algonquian Indians, which serves as an example to show how legends may reflect the beliefs, fears, and hopes of a specific culture. Illustrated by appropriate and informative line drawings. Ages 10-12.

LENT, BLAIR. *John Tabor's Ride*. Illustrated by Blair Lent. Boston: Atlantic Monthly Press, 1966.

John Tabor is rescued from a South Sea island by a strange, bearded man and is brought back to New England on the back of a whale. Three-color watercolor prints made from cardboard cutouts illustrate this humorous whaling legend. Ages 6-10.

LEWIS, RICHARD, ed. *Out of the Earth I Sing*. New York: W. W. Norton & Company, Inc., 1968.

An anthology of poetry and songs of primitive peoples of the world. Human concerns and emotions expressed by North American and South American Indians, African, Asian, Pacific, and Arctic cultures. Illustrations consist of well-produced and attractively arranged reproductions of primitive art pieces. Ages 10 and up.

LEXAU, JOAN M. *Every Day a Dragon*. Illustrated by Ben Shecter. New York: Harper & Row, Publishers, 1967.

A little boy and his father play a daily game of make-believe, and his mother's invitation to dinner saves him from being eaten by "a fierce dragon." Illustrated with sketches. Ages 3-5.

———. *Striped Ice Cream*. Illustrated by John Wilson. Philadelphia: J. B. Lippincott Co., 1968.

Realistic portrayal of situations faced by a self-reliant, fatherless Negro family. Black and white sketches highlight the genuine lifelike emotions depicted in this story. Ages 6-10.

LIFTON, BETTY JEAN. *The Dwarf Pine Tree*. Illustrated by Fuko-Akino. New York: Atheneum Publishers, 1963.

After it has endured months of torturous pain and learns that it will have only six months left on earth, a small straight-as-a-stick pine tree is chosen as the tree that is used to cure a princess of her mysterious malady. Illustrations are beautifully compatible with this moving Japanese folktale. Ages 8-12.

———. *The Rice-cake Rabbit*. Illustrated by Eiichi Mitsui. New York: W. W. Norton & Company, Inc., 1966.

A fantasy based on a Japanese folktale about a rabbit, successful baker of rice-cakes, who becomes a master at swordsmanship and is made Samurai of the Moon. Stunning brush and black ink sketches illustrate this tale. Ages 6-9.

———. *The Secret Seller*. Illustrated with photographs and drawings by Etienne Delessert. New York: W. W. Norton & Company, Inc., 1968.

A lonely little boy has everything except a secret, but finds a great one while sitting on a bench in Central Park. Illustrated effectively with black and white photographs and stylized drawings in four colors. Ages 5-9.

LINDGREN, ASTRID. *The Tomten*. Illustrated by Harold Wiberg. New York: Coward-McCann, Inc., 1961.

An adaptation of Viktor Rydberg's poem about Tomten, a character from Swedish folklore, who wanders around at night talking to animals and looking in on families while they sleep. Illustrations are stunning pictures done in a rather decorative and representational style with muted colors. Ages 5-7.

LIONNI, LEO. *The Biggest House in the World.* Illustrated by Leo Lionni. New York: Pantheon Books, Inc., 1968.

After hearing how one snail grew to such an enormous size that he was unable to move about from cabbage to cabbage and thus slowly faded way, a little snail appreciates his small size and the movability of his house. Illustrations are large colorful and imaginative paintings. Ages 4-8.

———. *Frederick.* Illustrated by Leo Lionni. New York: Pantheon Books, Inc., 1967.

Frederick recreates the wonder of the seasons through the magic of imagery language, whereas the other members of a hardworking field mouse family gather food for the winter. Illustrated with three-dimensional collage pictures. Ages 5-8.

———. *Tico and the Golden Wings.* Illustrated by Leo Lionni. New York: Pantheon Books, Inc., 1964.

An Indian folktale about a bird who gives away his golden feathers to bring happiness to those in need; and although he looks like all the other black birds, he knows he is different for he has his own memories and dreams. Illustrated in muted colors in a style suggestive of the traditional art of India. Ages 5-10.

LIPKIND, WILLIAM. *The Two Reds.* Illustrated by Nicolas Mordvinoff. New York: Harcourt, Brace & World, Inc., 1950.

The two reds, a boy and a cat, are faced with a common danger and become friends. Illustrations are stylized drawings with clever red accents. Ages 6-8.

MATSUNO, MASAKO. *A Pair of Red Clogs.* Illustrated by Kazue Mizumura. Cleveland: The World Publishing Company, 1960.

A little Japanese girl cracks her new red clogs and tries to deceive her mother by walking in the mud. Illustrated with simple and effective sketches that convey the emotions and actions of the characters. Ages 5-7.

MATTHIESEN, THOMAS. *A B C; an Alphabet Book.* Photographs by Thomas Matthiesen. New York: Platt & Munk, Inc., 1966.

Colored photographs of familiar objects (shoes, keys, a clock, etc.) and simple text present the twenty-six letters of the alphabet. Ages 3-6.

———. *Things to See.* Photographs by Thomas Matthiesen. New York: Platt & Munk, Inc., 1966.

Colored photographs and simple text are used to identify objects common in a child's world. Ages 3-6.

MCCLOSKEY, ROBERT. *Make Way for Ducklings.* Illustrated by Robert McCloskey. New York: The Viking Press, Inc., 1941.

A large picture book which tells the story about a family of ducks that grew up in the Boston area. Representational drawings highlight the laughable situations and portray some familiar Bostonian landmarks. Ages 4-8.

———. *Time of Wonder.* Illustrated by Robert McCloskey. New York: The Viking Press, Inc., 1957.

A description of the many moods and interesting terrain of the Maine Coast, in poetic prose and full-color watercolor paintings. Ages 7-12.

Also Worthy of Note:

McCLOSKEY, ROBERT. *One Morning in Maine.* New York: The Viking Press, Inc., 1952. Ages 5-9.

McNEER, MAY. *America's Abraham Lincoln.* Illustrated by Lynd Ward. Boston: Houghton Mifflin Company, 1957.

A biography covering the life of Lincoln from age seven to his assassination. Black and white, and colored lithographs done in a representational art style illustrate the biography. Ages 10-14.

Also Worthy of Note:

McNEER, MAY. *The American Indian Story.* Illustrated by Lynd Ward. New York: Farrar, Straus & Giroux, Inc., 1963. Ages 10-14.

MERRILL, JEAN. *Red Riding.* Illustrated by Ronni Solbert. New York: Pantheon Books, a division of Random House, Inc., 1968.

The story of *Red Ridinghood* is "revised and updated" to reflect a modern setting. It is told by a little girl to entertain her brother on a rainy day. Childlike drawings in bright flat colors illustrate the story. Ages 4-7.

MINCIELI, ROSE LAURA. *Old Neopolitan Fairy Tales.* Illustrated by Beni Montresor. New York: Alfred A. Knopf, Inc., 1963.

A compilation of ten Italian folktales (retold from *Il Pentamerone*), including the Italian versions of *Cinderella, Rapunzel,* and *The Three Citrons.* Illustrations are black and white line drawings which comply with the mood and content of these romantic tales. Ages 8-12.

MONTGOMERY, RUTHERFORD. *Kildee House.* Illustrated by Barbara Cooney. Garden City, N.Y.: Doubleday & Company, Inc., 1949.

Jerome's plan for a hermit's lazy existence on a mountainside is drastically changed when he shares his house with a *pair* of raccoons and a *pair* of skunks. Charming illustrations extend this delightful animal story and help to make it even more enjoyable. Ages 9-12.

MOORE, LILLIAN. *I Feel the Same Way.* Illustrated by Robert Quackenbush. New York: Atheneum Publishers, 1967.

A compilation of twenty short poems which are characterized by simplicity in imagery, and which interpret childlike responses to the world of nature and to personal experiences. Illustrated with pictures in soft pastels. Ages 3-7.

MUNARI, BRUNO. *The Birthday Present.* Illustrated by Bruno Munari. Cleveland: The World Publishing Company, 1959.

A "participation" picture book in which various means of transportation are used to bring a birthday present to a three-year-old boy. Illustrated with bold but simple flat-colored pictures done with tempera. Ages 3-5.

NESS, EVALINE. *Sam, Bangs and Moonshine.* Illustrated by Evaline Ness. New York: Holt, Rinehart & Winston, Inc., 1966.

Sam, a fisherman's daughter, gets her friend, Thomas, and her cat, Bangs, into serious difficulties as a result of her tall tales ("moonshine"). Illustrated effectively with line and wash drawings. Recipient of 1967 Caldecott Medal. Ages 5-8.

———. *Tom Tit Tot.* Illustrated by Evaline Ness. New York: Charles Scribner's Sons, 1965.

An English version of the well-known fairy tale, Rumpelstiltskin, presented in picture book form. Illustrations are woodcuts done in black, blue, and brown shades and emphasize the humor of this tale. Ages 5-8.

Also Worthy of Note:

NESS, EVALINE. *Josephina February.* Illustrated by Evaline Ness. New York: Charles Scribner's Sons, 1963. Ages 5-7.

NEWBERRY, CLARE TURLAY. *April's Kittens.* Illustrated by Clare Turlay Newberry. New York: Harper & Row, Publishers, 1940.

Six-year-old April has to decide how to part with three kittens, offsprings of her own cat, Sheba. Appealing black and white charcoal drawings are representational in style and masterfully portray the playful antics of the kittens. Ages 5-7.

NIC LEODHAS, SORCHE. (pseud. Alger LeClaire). *All in the Morning Early.* Illustrated by Evaline Ness. New York: Holt, Rinehart & Winston, Inc., 1963.

A retelling of an old Scottish nursery rhyme . . . a boy on his way to a mill is joined by one huntsman winding his horn, two old ewes by the shepard shorn, etc. Two- and-four-color drawings illustrate this tale which is told in poetic prose and couplets. Ages 5-9.

———. *Always Room for One More.* Illustrated by Nonny Hogrogian. New York: Holt, Rinehart & Winston, Inc., 1965.

A picture book version of an old Scottish folk song about a hospitable man who fills his house with guests until their gaiety causes it to tumble down. Illustrations are black and white pen and line drawings with touches of pastels in heather and green for the fields to convey the fresh atmosphere and beauty of Scotland. Recipient of the 1966 Caldecott Medal. Ages 5-9.

NUSSBAUMER, MARES. *Away in a Manger; A Story of the Nativity.* Illustrated by Paul Nussbaumer. New York: Harcourt, Brace & World, Inc., 1965.

An expanded version of the story of the nativity (set in Switzerland). Illustrated with full-color poster paintings. Musical scores for "Away in a Manger" and "O Come Little Children" are included. Ages 5-9.

OBERHANSLI, TRUDI. *Sleep Baby, Sleep; An Old Cradle Song.* Illustrated by Trudi Oberhansli. New York: Atheneum Publishers, 1967.

A picture book version of an old German lullaby. The melody is given at the end. Illustrated with pictures done in childlike, primitive style in vibrant shades. Ages 2-5.

PERRINE, MARY. *Salt Boy.* Illustrated by Leonard Weisgard. New York: Abelard-Schuman, Limited, 1968.

A Navajo Indian boy is forced to lasso a lamb that is swept away in a flash flood. Illustrated in three colors in drawings suggestive of primitive art. Ages 5-8.

PIATTI, CELESTINO. *Celestino Piatti's Animal A B C.* English text by Jon Reid. Illustrated by Celestino Piatti. New York: Atheneum Publishers, 1966.

For each letter of the alphabet, four-line rhymes identify animals from alligator to zebra. Bold drawings that are brightly-colored poster paintings illustrate this alphabet book. Ages 3-6.

PILKINGTON, FRANCIS M. *The Three Sorrowful Tales of Erin.* Illustrated by Victor Ambrus. New York: Henry Z. Walck, Inc., 1966.

Three Irish legends telling about the punishment given three murderers and the tragic destiny of the children of Lir and Deirdre. Drawings reflect the harsh and heroic mood and setting of the legends, which originated around the third century. Ages 11-14.

PLOTZ, HELEN. *Imagination's Other Place.* Illustrated by Clare Leighton. New York: Thomas Y. Crowell Company, 1955.

An anthology of poetry about aspects of science and mathematics. Illustrated with symbolic wood engravings printed in black and white. Ages 12 and up.

POLITI, LEO. *Song of the Swallows.* Illustrated by Leo Politi. New York: Charles Scribner's Sons, 1949.

A little boy in the California town of Capistrano, an old gardener, and the bell ringer at the Mission of San Juan Capistrano welcome the swallows as they fly in from the sea on St. Joseph's day. Illustrated with full-color watercolor paintings; figures are primitive and lumbering. Ages 5-8.

Also Worthy of Note:

POLITI, LEO. *Pedro, the Angel of Olvera Street.* New York: Charles Scribner's Sons, 1946. Ages 5-7.

RAND, ANN and PAUL. *I Know a Lot of Things.* Illustrated by Paul Rand. New York: Harcourt, Brace & World, Inc., 1956.

A child is helped to notice and view the world around him with an attitude of wonder and delight. Illustrations are bright-colored impressionistic drawings. Ages 4-6.

Also Worthy of Note:

RAND, ANN and PAUL. *Sparkle and Spin.* New York: Harcourt, Brace & World, Inc., 1957. Deals with words—meanings, use, and sounds. Ages 4-8.

RAVIELLI, ANTHONY. *Wonders of the Human Body.* Illustrated by Anthony Ravielli. New York: The Viking Press, Inc., 1954.

The structure of the human body is explained by comparing it to a machine. Graphic and imaginative drawings are anatomically accurate and explicit. Ages 10-14.

Also Worthy of Note:

RAVIELLI, ANTHONY. *The World is Round.* Illustrated by Anthony Ravielli. New York: The Viking Press, Inc., 1963. Ages 7-12.

REED, PHILIP, ed. *Mother Goose and Nursery Rhymes.* New York: Atheneum Publishers, 1963.

An anthology of carefully selected nursery rhymes, illustrated with colored wood engravings in a quaint style suggestive of the eighteenth century. Ages 4-8.

RIDDELL, JAMES. *Hit or Myth.* Illustrated by James Riddell. New York: Harper & Row, Publishers, 1949, 1969.

An unusual format; the pages of this book are divided in half horizontally so that the reader can form many different kinds of creatures, (some real and some fanciful) by combining the upper and lower halves of the animals in whatever ways he wishes. Ages 5-10.

RINGI, KJELL. *The Magic Stick.* Illustrated by Kjell Ringi. New York: Harper & Row, Publishers, 1968.

Picture book without words. Brilliantly colored pictures depict the things a little boy imagines he can become—a pirate with a telescope, a weight-lifter, and a general leading a parade. Ages 4-7.

RITCHIE, JEAN. *Apple Seeds and Soda Straws.* Illustrated by Don Bolognese. New York: Henry Z. Walck, Inc., 1965.

A compilation of love charms and legends collected in Appalachian Mountain area. Pen-and-ink drawings done in cartoon style highlight the lively humor of these superstitious sayings and practices. Ages 8-12.

ROBBINS, RUTH. *Baboushka and the Three Kings.* Illustrated by Nicolas Sidjakov. Berkeley: Parnassus Press, 1960.

An adaptation of a Russian folktale about an old woman who searches for the Christ child. Illustrated in brilliantly-colored stylized drawings done in tempera and felt pen. Awarded the 1961 Caldecott Medal. Ages 7-10.

Also Worthy of Note:

ROBBINS, RUTH. *The Emperor and the Drummer Boy.* Illustrated by Nicolas Sidjakov. Berkeley: Parnassus Press, 1962. Ages 9-12.

ROUNDS, GLEN. *The Boll Weevil.* Illustrations by Glen Rounds. Los Angeles: Golden Gate Junior Books, 1967.

A picture book presentation of a familiar southern ballad that tells of a farmer's losing battle with the boll weevil. The faintly-colored drawings are rustic, and emphasize the wry humor of the ballad. Ages 6-11.

——— *Wild Horses of the Red Desert.* Illustrated by Glen Rounds. New York: Holiday House, Inc., 1969.

A matter-of-fact description of the activities, trials, and tribulations of the wild horses that roam the Red Desert, an area of "rocky ridges, twisting canyons, and dusty sagebrush flats." Drawings done in rough brush line effectively convey the wildness, spaciousness, and challenging setting of this story. Ages 9-14.

SANDBURG, CARL. *The Wedding Procession of the Rag Doll and the Broom Handle and Who Was in It*. Illustrated by Harriet Pincus. New York: Harcourt, Brace & World, Inc., 1967.

A picture book version of a tale from Sandburg's *The Rootabaga Stories*. Unique and imaginative drawings reflect the humor of the story. Ages 6-9.

SASEK, MIROSLAV. *This is New York*. Illustrated by Miroslav Sasek. New York: The Macmillan Company, 1960.

A sophisticated view of typical landmarks and scenes of New York City. Illustrated with stylized drawings and pointillism. Ages 8-13.

SCHACKBURG, RICHARD. *Yankee Doodle* (Song). Illustrated by Ed Emberley. Notes by Barbara Emberley. Englewood Cliffs, N.J.: Prentice-Hall, Inc., 1965.

A colorful picture book interpretation of this ten-verse song about the Yankee soldiers during the Revolutionary War. Illustrations are precise and striking full-color woodcuts. Included are simple arrangements for the verses, brief historical notes about the song, and a recipe for hasty pudding. Ages 4-7.

SCHATZ, LETTA. *Bolla and the Oba's Drummers*. Illustrated by Tom Feelings. New York: McGraw-Hill Book Company, 1967.

An account of a talented drummer who became an apprentice for the Oba's Royal Drummers. Black and white tempera paintings convey the mood and depict the West African setting. Ages 10-13.

SCHEER, JULIAN. *Rain Makes Applesauce*. Illustrated by Marvin Bileck. New York: Holiday House, Inc., 1964.

A series of wonderfully nonsensical ideas and the refrains ". . . and rain makes applesauce" and "oh, you just talking silly talk." Intricate and imaginative drawings in pale colors match the nonsense of the text. A careful observer will notice that indeed rain does make applesauce, for the artist has shown, step by step, that from a seedling come bushels of apples with which delicious applesauce is made. Ages 4-8.

SCHOENHERR, JOHN. *The Barn*. Illustrated by John Schoenherr. Boston: Little, Brown and Company, 1968.

A skunk experiences terror when he becomes the prey of a great horned owl during a severe summer drought. Illustrated with black and white representational drawings. Ages 7-12.

SEIDELMAN, JAMES E. and MINTONYE, GRACE. *The 14th Dragon*. (Drawings by 13 illustrators). New York: Harlin Quist Books, 1968.

A clever narrative verse that describes the thirteen kinds of dragons found by hunters—the fourteenth dragon is created by the reader. Each of the thirteen dragons was drawn by a different artist. They used full color and a variety of media. Ages 4-10.

SENDAK, MAURICE. *Hector Protector* and *As I Went Over the Water*. Illustrated by Maurice Sendak. New York: Harper & Row, Publishers, 1965.

Two nursery rhymes imaginatively and playfully illustrated with cartoon-type drawings. Ages 3-6.

————. *The Nutshell Library.* Illustrated by Maurice Sendak. New York: Harper & Row, Publishers, 1962.

A set of four nonsense picture books: *Alligators All Around* (an alphabet book), *Chicken Soup with Rice* (a book about the months), *One Was Johnny* (a counting book), and *Pierre* (a cautionary tale in five chapters and a prologue). Illustrated with delightfully humorous cartoon-style sketches. Ages 4-8.

————. *Where the Wild Things Are.* Illustrated by Maurice Sendak. New York: Harper & Row, Publishers, 1963.

A playful fanciful tale about a boy in a wolf suit who sails away to where the wild things are. Illustrations are imaginative, colorful cartoon-style paintings. Excellent use of color and white space to designate the boy's involvement in fantasy and reality. Ages 4-8.

Also Worthy of Note:

SENDAK, MAURICE. *Higglety, Pigglety, Pop! Or, There Must be More to Life.* Illustrated by Maurice Sendak. New York: Harper & Row, Publishers, 1967. Ages 5-8.

SEUSS, DR. *The 500 Hats of Bartholomew Cubbins.* New York: Vanguard Press, Inc., 1938.

A folktale-type story about a small boy who enrages the king because he doesn't (cannot) remove his hat. Effective cartoon-style illustrations match the hilarious story. Ages 5-12.

Also Worthy of Note:

SEUSS, DR. *Horton Hatches the Egg.* Illustrated by Dr. Seuss. New York: Random House, Inc., 1940. Ages 5-10.

SHOWALTER, JEAN B. *The Donkey Ride.* Illustrated by Tomi Ungerer. Garden City, N.Y.: Doubleday & Company, Inc., 1967.

A farmer takes the advice of everyone he meets on the way to market until he and his son are dumped into the river while trying to carry their donkey across a bridge. Humorous illustrations add to the absurdity of events related in this extended version of a familiar fable. Ages 6-10.

SHULEVITZ, URI. *One Monday Morning.* Illustrated by Uri Shulevitz. New York: Charles Scribner's Sons, 1967.

A little boy living in a dreary tenement building pretends that a king, a queen, and a little prince had visited him repeatedly during the course of a week, but were able to find him at home only on Sunday. Charming colorful illustrations depict the repetitious story. Ages 4-8.

SIMON, NORMA. *What Do I Say?* Illustrated by Joe Lasker. Chicago: Albert Whitman & Co., 1967.

The typical day of a little Puerto Rican boy living in a large American city is portrayed: what he says when he gets up in the morning, when he leaves for school, when asked his name, and other situations. Illustrations are colored, and black and white. (Also available in an English-Spanish edition.) Ages 4-6.

SINGER, ISAAC BASHEVIS. *The Fearsome Inn.* Illustrated by Nonny Hogrogian. New York: Charles Scribner's Sons, 1967.

An exciting account of a young man's using a piece of magic chalk to save himself, his two friends, and three beautiful girls from a wicked witch and her half-devil husband who hold them captive in an inn. Distinctive full-color illustrations interpret mood, characters, and events. Ages 8-12.

———. *Mazel and Shlimazel or The Milk of a Lioness.* Illustrated by Margot Zemach. Translated by the author and Elizabeth Shub. New York: Farrar, Straus & Giroux, Inc., 1967.

A Yiddish fairy tale about Mazel, the spirit of good luck, and Shlimazel, the spirit of bad luck, who vie with each other over the fate of a peasant boy. Full-color illustrations are suggestive of eastern European peasant art. Ages 7-10.

———. *Zlateh, the Goat, and Other Stories.* Illustrated by Maurice Sendak. Translated by Isaac Singer and Elizabeth Shub. New York: Harper & Row, Publishers, 1966.

A compilation of seven wise and humorous Yiddish folktales. The black and white drawings very effectively convey the old middle European atmosphere of the stories. Ages 10-14.

SMUCKER, BARBARA C. *Wigwam in the City.* Illustrated by Gil Miret. New York: E. P. Dutton & Co., Inc., 1966.

A sober account of the experiences and emotions of a twelve-year-old Chippewa Indian girl and her family when they leave their impoverished reservation to live and work in Chicago. Although there are only a few woodcut prints included to illustrate this story, they highlight the major events and atmosphere extremely well. Ages 10-13.

SPIER, PETER. *London Bridge Is Falling Down.* Illustrated by Peter Spier. Garden City, N.Y.: Doubleday & Company, Inc., 1967.

A picture book version of the well-known nursery song. Includes many verses plus a brief history of the bridge and music for the song. Illustrated with colorful, detailed drawings that present some well-known landmarks of London. Ages 5-8.

STEVENSON, ROBERT LOUIS. *A Child's Garden of Verses.* Illustrated by Brian Wildsmith. New York: Franklin Watts, Inc., 1966.

Colorful stylized paintings illustrate this compilation of familiar poems by Robert Louis Stevenson. Ages 4-9.

STOCKTON, FRANK R. *The Bee Man of Orn.* Illustrated by Maurice Sendak. New York: Holt, Rinehart & Winston, Inc., 1965.

A satirical fantasy about a bee man who sets out to discover his original form. Illustrated with colored cartoon-style drawings that match the humor of the story. Ages 8-12.

SUBA, SUSANNE. *The Man with the Bushy Beard.* Illustrated by Susanne Suba. New York: The Viking Press, Inc., 1969.

A compilation of five short folktales from eastern Europe. The watercolor paintings that illustrate these tales are large and robust. They emphasize the stupidity of the action and the lack of thoughtfulness that is stressed in each tale. Ages 4-8.

TEAL, VALENTINE. *The Little Woman Wanted Noise.* Illustrated by Robert Lawson. Chicago: Rand McNally & Co., 1967.

A woman moves out to the country to get away from the noises of the city but gradually gathers a menagerie of things that make noise. Illustrated with line sketches that highlight the humor of the story. Ages 4-7.

TENNYSON, ALFRED LORD. *The Charge of the Light Brigade.* Illustrated by Alice and Martin Provensen. New York: Golden Press, Inc., 1964.

A picture book version of the well-known poem which commemorates the disastrous British cavalry charge against the Russian batteries in 1854. Stunning double-page, full-color gouache paintings interpret this poem. Ages 8-14.

THAYER, ERNEST L. *The First Book Edition of Casey at the Bat.* Illustrated by Leonard Everett Fisher. (Introduction by Casey Stengel.) New York: Franklin Watts, Inc., 1964.

A picture book version of the well-known narrative poem. Illustrated with effective scratchboard drawings in black and white. Ages 10-15.

THOMPSON, GEORGE SELDEN. *Sparrow Socks.* Illustrated by Peter Lippman. New York: Harper & Row, Publishers, 1965.

A young boy uses his family's knitting machine to make warm socks for the shivering sparrows, and soon every person in town wants to own a pair of "sparrow socks." Illustrations are detailed black and white sketches with clever red accents throughout. Ages 4-9.

THOMPSON, VIVIAN. *Hawaiian Myths of Earth, Sea and Sky.* Illustrated by Leonard Weisgard. New York: Holiday House, Inc., 1966.

A compilation of twelve ancient Polynesian-Hawaiian folktales pertaining to the origin of the world, to the seasons, and to the natural wonders of the Hawaiian Islands. Black, green, and red drawings illustrate the setting and action of the tales. Ages 9-12.

TRESSELT, ALVIN. *Hide and Seek Fog.* Illustrated by Roger Duvoisin. New York: Lothrop, Lee & Shepard Co., Inc., 1965.

A mood picture book describing the fog as it rolls in from the sea to veil an Atlantic seacoast village. Exquisite expressionistic paintings done in gouache illustrate this book. Ages 4-8.

TRESSELT, ALVIN, and CLEAVER, NANCY. *The Legend of the Willow Plate.* Illustrated by Joseph Low. New York: Parents' Magazine Press, 1968.

The tragic love story of the highborn Koong-se and the poor peasant poet, Chang, is the tale behind the Chinese scene that is depicted on the famous blue and white willow-pattern dinnerware, and the topic of this picture book. Illustrated with line drawings colored in soft-hued shades. Ages 6-10.

Also Worthy of Note:

TRESSELT, ALVIN. *"Hi, Mister Robin!"* Illustrated by Roger Duvoisin. New York: Lothrop, Lee & Shepard Co., Inc., 1950. Ages 4-8.

TRESSELT, ALVIN. *White Snow, Bright Snow.* Illustrated by Roger Duvoisin. New York: Lothrop, Lee & Shepard Co., Inc., 1947. Ages 4-8.

TRESSELT, ALVIN. *World in the Candy Egg.* Illustrated by Roger Duvoisin. New York: Lothrop, Lee & Shepard Co., Inc., 1967. Ages 4-8.

TUDOR, TASHA. *First Delights; A Book about the Five Senses.* Illustrated by Tasha Tudor. New York: Platt & Munk, Inc., 1966.

A little girl who lives on a farm discovers and enjoys through her senses the wonders and pleasures of the different seasons of the year. Realistic watercolor paintings in full color extend the brief text. Ages 5-7.

———. *Take Joy! The Tasha Tudor Christmas Book.* Illustrated by Tasha Tudor. Cleveland: The World Publishing Company, 1966.

A compilation of thoughts, poems, stories, lore, and legend focusing on Christmas, plus a description of the Tudors' own Christmas celebration. Illustrated with black and white drawings and full-color watercolor paintings. Ages 3-7.

Also Worthy of Note:

TUDOR TASHA, *A Is for Annabelle.* Illustrated by Tasha Tudor. New York: Henry Z. Walck, Inc., 1954. Ages 4-6.

UCHIDA, YOSHIKO. *Sumi's Special Happening.* Illustrated by Kazue Mizumura. New York: Charles Scribner's Sons, 1966.

A little Japanese girl presents her ninety-nine-year-old friend with a birthday gift he will not soon forget—a ride on the village's fire engine jeep with the bells and siren sounding out loud and clear. Illustrations are colored drawings that highlight the Japanese setting. Ages 6-9.

UDRY, JANICE. *What Mary Jo Shared.* Illustrations by Eleanor Mill. Chicago: Albert Whitman & Company, 1966.

A shy little kindergartener brings her father to school as part of the Sharing Time activity. Illustrated effectively with realistic colored and black and white drawings. Ages 5-8.

UNGERER, TOMI. *Moon Man.* Illustrated by Tomi Ungerer. New York: Harper & Row, Publishers, 1967.

Shortly after Moon Man descends to earth on the fiery tale of a comet, he is captured and imprisoned but is able to escape by means of special lunar powers. Eventually, he returns to the moon in a spacecraft. Bold drawings in strong colors illustrate this humorous fantasy. Ages 4-8.

———. *Zeralda's Ogre.* Illustrated by Tomi Ungerer. New York: Harper & Row, Publishers, 1967.

The dietary habits of a child-eating ogre are changed so that he learns to enjoy roast turkey á la Cinderella, chocolate sauce Rasputin, and other such appetizing concoctions. Illustrations are droll sketches in vivid colors. Ages 5-8.

VALENS, EVANS G. *Wildfire.* Illustrated by Clement Hurd. Cleveland: The World Publishing Company, 1963.

A moving account of the reactions of the birds and animals of the forest to a fire caused by lightning. The story tells how life in the forest is resumed again after the fire. Illustrated with woodcuts printed on rice paper. Ages 9-12.

VARNER, VELMA. *The Animal Frolic.* Illustrated by Kakuyu (pseud., Toba Sojo). New York: G. P. Putnam's Sons, 1967.

Picture book form reproduction of a thirty-six foot scroll, entitled "Choju Giga" or "Scroll of Animals," an early masterpiece of Japanese art and humor. The pictures of animals playing and feasting in the forest are done in caricature art style and are printed in duotone. Ages 5-9.

WABER, BERNARD. *An Anteater Named Arthur*. Illustrated by Bernard Waber. Boston: Houghton Mifflin Company, 1967.

Arthur, an anteater, is messy, choosy, bored, curious, and loveable. Illustrations are droll cartoon style sketches colored in pink and brown. Ages 4-8.

———. *Lyle and the Birthday Party*. Illustrated by Bernard Waber. Boston: Houghton Mifflin Company, 1966.

Lyle, usually an amiable crocodile, suddenly becomes despondent and overcome with jealousy during a birthday party. He is sent to the hospital where he forgets his jealousy by helping others. Illustrated with superb cartoon-style sketches. Ages 4-8.

WARD, LYND. *The Biggest Bear*. Illustrated by Lynd Ward. Boston: Houghton Mifflin Company, 1952.

A dramatic account of a little bear that grew to be a big bear and a nuisance to the valley. The realistic sepia drawings portray the compassion, humor, and suspense of this story amazingly well. Ages 4-8.

WEIK, MARY HAYS. *The Jazz Man*. Illustrated by Ann Grifalconi. New York: Atheneum Publishers, 1966.

Nine-year-old Zeke lives in an old brownstone house in Harlem. How he spends his day, the warm relationship that exists between Zeke and his parents, and his temporary abandonment by his parents are related realistically and with exquisite poetic prose. Superb expressionistic woodcuts illustrate this sensitive imagery-filled narrative. Ages 7-11.

WILDSMITH, BRIAN. *Brian Wildsmith's Birds*. Illustrated by Brian Wildsmith. New York: Franklin Watts, Inc., 1967.

A compilation of double-spread pictures of brilliantly colored groups of birds identified by clever single-lined captions. Illustrations are poster paintings. Ages 4-9.

WILDSMITH, BRIAN. *Hare and the Tortoise*. Illustrated by Brian Wildsmith. New York: Franklin Watts, Inc., 1967.

A picture book interpretation of La Fontaine's fable about the race between the hare and the tortoise. Imaginative and bright-colored paintings depict the humor and action of this well-known fable. Ages 5-9.

Also Worthy of Note:

WILDSMITH, BRIAN. *Brian Wildsmith's Fishes*. Illustrated by Brian Wildsmith. New York: Franklin Watts, Inc., 1968. Ages 4-9.

———. *Brian Wildsmith's 1, 2, 3's*. Illustrated by Brian Wildsmith. New York: Franklin Watts, Inc., 1965. Ages 4-9.

———. *Brian Wildsmith's Wild Animals*. Illustrated by Brian Wildsmith. New York: Franklin Watts, Inc., 1967. Ages 4-9.

WYNDHAM, ROBERT. *Chinese Mother Goose Rhymes*. Illustrated by Ed Young. Cleveland: The World Publishing Company, 1968.

A collection of Mandarin Chinese nursery rhymes, riddles, games, and nonsense verses. Illustrated with paintings suggestive of classical Chinese art. The original Chinese version of each rhyme is also presented in Chinese calligraphy. The book is to be read vertically like an oriental scroll. Ages 5-9.

YASHIMA, TARO. *Crow Boy.* Illustrated by Taro Yashima. New York: The Viking Press, Inc., 1955.

An expressive picture book account of a lonely little Japanese boy who attends a village school, is ridiculed and ignored by his classmates, but who is eventually appreciated for his unique talent. Illustrated with expressionistic full-color paintings done in brush and pencil. Ages 5-9.

YASHIMA, TARO. *Umbrella.* Illustrated by Taro Yashima. New York: The Viking Press, Inc., 1958. Ages 4-6.

Also Worthy of Note:

YASHIMA, TARO. *Seashore.* Illustrated by Taro Yashima. New York: The Viking Press, Inc., 1967. Ages 6-10.

YOLEN, JANE H. *The Emperor and the Kite.* Illustrated by Ed Young. Cleveland: The World Publishing Company, 1967.

Princess Djeow Seow, an oft-forgotten daughter of a Chinese emperor, through her love and cleverness, keeps her father alive and rescues him by means of her kite when he is imprisoned in a tower in the middle of a treeless plain. Illustrated with pictures cut from a single piece of paper, a technique typical of a traditional art form. Ages 6-9.

ZEMACH, HARVE. *Mommy, Buy Me a China Doll.* Illustrated by Margot Zemach. Chicago: Follett Publishing Company, 1966.

Humorous cumulative verse pertaining to ridiculous swapping of sleeping places after Eliza Lou suggests that her Daddy made his feather bed in order to get her a china doll. Illustrated in line and wash drawings that emphasize the folk quality of this Ozark Mountain area children's song. Ages 4-8.

Also Worthy of Note:

ZEMACH, HARVE. *Nail Soup.* Illustrated by Margot Zemach. Chicago: Follett Publishing Company, 1964. Ages 4-6.

———. *Salt.* Illustrated by Margot Zemach. Chicago: Follett Publishing Company, 1965.

———. *The Speckled Hen: a Russian Nursery Rhyme.* Illustrated by Margot Zemach. New York: Holt, Rinehart & Winston, Inc., 1966. Ages 4-6.

———. *Too Much Nose.* Illustrated by Margot Zemach. New York: Holt, Rinehart & Winston, Inc., 1967. Ages 6-7.

ZOLOTOW, CHARLOTTE. *Big Sister and Little Sister.* Illustrated by Martha Alexander. New York: Harper & Row, Publishers, 1966.

Two sisters learn to take care of one another. Illustrated with pleasant, realistic drawings in delicate shades of pink and green. Ages 4-7.

selected professional references

BRUNNER, FELIX. *A Handbook of Graphic Reproduction Processes.* New York: Hastings House, Publishers, Inc., 1968.

BLAND, DAVID. *The Illustration of Books.* London: Faber & Faber, Ltd., 1962.

COLBY, JEAN POINDEXTER. *Writing, Illustrating and Editing Children's Books.* New York: Hastings House, Publishers, Inc., 1967.

CROY, PETER. *Graphic Design and Reproduction Techniques.* New York: Hastings House, Publishers, Inc., 1968.

HUCK, CHARLOTTE S., and KUHN, DORIS YOUNG. *Children's Literature in the Elementary School.* New York: Holt, Rinehart & Winston, Inc., 1968.

KINGMAN, LEE; FOSTER, JOANNA; and LONTOFT, RUTH GILES. *Illustrators of Children's Books: 1957-1966.* Boston: Horn Book, Inc., 1968.

LEWIS, JOHN. *Twentieth Century Book, Its Illustration and Design.* New York: Reinhold Publishing Corp., 1967.

PITZ, HENRY C. *Illustrating Children's Books; History, Technique, Production.* New York: Watson-Guptill Publications, 1963.

REED, W., ed. *Illustrator in America, 1900-1960's.* New York: Reinhold Publishing Corp., 1967.

STONE, BERNARD, and ECKSTEIN, ARTHUR. *Preparing Art for Printing.* New York: Reinhold Publishing Corp., 1965.

WEITENKAMPF, FRANK. *The Illustrated Book.* Cambridge: Harvard University Press, 1938.

Periodicals:

American Artist
Elementary English
The Horn Book Magazine
Junior Bookshelf
Publishers' Weekly
School Librarian
Top of the News
The Writer

caldecott medal award books

The Caldecott Medal is awarded each year to the artist who has illustrated the most distinguished American picture book for children. The winner is selected by a committee of the Children's Services Division of the American Library Association.

1969 THE FOOL OF THE WORLD AND THE FLYING SHIP, by Arthur Ransome. Illustrated by Uri Shulevitz. New York: Farrar, Straus & Giroux, Inc., 1968.

1968 DRUMMER HOFF, by Barbara Emberley. Illustrated by Ed Emberley. Englewood Cliffs, N.J.: Prentice-Hall, Inc., 1967.

1967 SAM, BANGS AND MOONSHINE, written and illustrated by Evaline Ness. New York: Holt, Rinehart & Winston, Inc., 1966.

1966 ALWAYS ROOM FOR ONE MORE, by Sorche Nic Leodhas. Illustrated by Nonny Hogrogian. New York: Holt, Rinehart & Winston, Inc., 1965.

1965 MAY I BRING A FRIEND?, by Beatrice Schenk de Regniers. Illustrated by Beni Montresor. New York: Atheneum Publishers, 1964.

1964 WHERE THE WILD THINGS ARE, written and illustrated by Maurice Sendak. New York: Harper & Row, Publishers, 1963.

1963 THE SNOWY DAY, written and illustrated by Ezra Jack Keats. New York: The Viking Press, Inc., 1962.

1962 ONCE A MOUSE, written and illustrated by Marcia Brown. New York: Charles Scribner's Sons, 1961.

1961 BABOUSHKA AND THE THREE KINGS, by Ruth Robbins. Illustrated by Nicolas Sidjakov. Berkeley: Parnassus Press, 1960.

1960 NINE DAYS TO CHRISTMAS, by Marie Hall Ets and Aurora Labastida. Illustrated by Marie Hall Ets. New York: The Viking Press, Inc., 1959.

1959 CHANTICLEER AND THE FOX, edited and illustrated by Barbara Cooney. New York: Thomas Y. Crowell Company, 1958.

1958 TIME OF WONDER, written and illustrated by Robert McCloskey. New York: The Viking Press, Inc., 1957.

1957 A TREE IS NICE, by Janice May Udry. Illustrated by Marc Simont. New York: Harper & Row, Publishers, 1956.

1956 FROG WENT A-COURTIN', by John Langstaff. Illustrated by Feodor Rojankovsky. New York: Harcourt, Brace & World, Inc., 1955.

1955 CINDERELLA, by Charles Perrault. Illustrated by Marcia Brown. New York: Charles Scribner's Sons, 1954.

1954 MADELINE'S RESCUE, written and illustrated by Ludwig Bemelmans. New York: The Viking Press, Inc., 1953.

1953 THE BIGGEST BEAR, written and illustrated by Lynd Ward. Boston: Houghton Mifflin Company, 1952.

1952 FINDERS KEEPERS, by Will and Nicolas (pseud. William Lipkind and Nicolas Mordvinoff). Illustrated by Nicolas. New York: Harcourt, Brace & World, Inc., 1951.

1951 THE EGG TREE, written and illustrated by Katherine Milhous. New York: Charles Scribner's Sons, 1950.

1950 SONG OF THE SWALLOWS, written and illustrated by Leo Politi. New York: Charles Scribner's Sons, 1949.

1949 THE BIG SNOW, written and illustrated by Berta and Elmer Hader. New York: The Macmillan Company, 1948.

1948 WHITE SNOW, BRIGHT SNOW, by Alvin Tresselt. Illustrated by Roger Duvoisin. New York: Lothrop, Lee & Shepard Co., Inc., 1947.

1947 THE LITTLE ISLAND, by Golden MacDonald. Illustrated by Leonard Weisgard. Garden City, N.Y.: Doubleday & Company, Inc., 1946.

1946 THE ROOSTER CROWS, by Maud and Miska Petersham. New York: The Macmillan Company, 1945.

1945 PRAYER FOR A CHILD, by Rachel Field. Illustrated by Elizabeth Orton Jones. New York: The Macmillan Company, 1944.

1944 MANY MOONS, by James Thurber. Illustrated by Louis Slobodkin. New York: Harcourt, Brace & World, Inc., 1943.

1943 THE LITTLE HOUSE, written and illustrated by Virginia Lee Burton. Boston: Houghton Mifflin Company, 1942.

1942 MAKE WAY FOR DUCKLINGS, written and illustrated by Robert McCloskey. New York: The Viking Press, Inc., 1941.

1941 THEY WERE STRONG AND GOOD, written and illustrated by Robert Lawson. New York: The Viking Press, Inc., 1940.

1940 ABRAHAM LINCOLN, written and illustrated by Ingri and Edgar D'Aulaire. Garden City, N.Y.: Doubleday & Company, Inc., 1939.

1939 MEI LEI, written and illustrated by Thomas Handforth. Garden City, N. Y.: Doubleday & Company, Inc., 1938.

1938 ANIMALS OF THE BIBLE, A PICTURE BOOK. Text selected from the King James Bible by Helen Dean Fish. Illustrated by Dorothy O. Lathrop. Philadelphia: Stokes (J. B. Lippincott Co.), 1937.

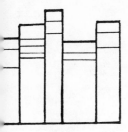

index